THE BEAST WITHIN

A COMPENDIUM OF MORPHS
AND OTHER CREATURES
OF THE NETHERWORLD

By
Dr. Tom Knotts Jr.
www.SRA-DIDFreedomInChrist.com

The Fall from Grace . . .

Sometimes in life we have encounters that science simply cannot explain, let alone identify. This book deals with one of those mysterious topics, anthropomorphism.[1] In conducting this study I was lead on a journey that took me into what can only be termed as the dark side of primitive man, the world of the supernatural.

The subject of shape shifting, a form of anthropomorphism, makes interesting reading for the curious mind but within the fabric of this so called realm of fantasy is the truth behind the myth. Shape shifting is a reality. Shape shifting occurs when another life force merges with a person's life force forming a symbiotic hybrid of conscious and spirit that becomes something other than human. For some it is a demonic curse from which there seems to be no escape. Others find the feeling of merging into another being quite enjoyable.

This book deals with the reality of the beast that is formed and the Netherworld that it inhabits. In the following pages you will find a map identifying the specific

---

[11] Anthropomorphism is the representation of a god, the ascription of human characteristics to things not human.

elements that are found within various groups of individuals composing the realm of the Netherworld. The Netherworld is defined as: the entire supernatural or magical community, which lives in, and upon the Earth with humanity, but one also that has access to the other places which cannot be bridged by normal means. By purity of definition this group would have a plethora of inhabitants possessing varying gifts and abilities. One inhabitant of this world is the person with the ability to astral project out of their body. Some people astral project out of their bodies at night while sleeping. Because they are asleep they have no idea that they possess this ability. Other people can project out of their bodies at will. Still others can only do it while in a meditative state. Astral projection allows a person to bridge the tangible/physical realm and enter into the spiritual/astral realm. Those with the ability to astral project have a spiritual gifting that is not common to mankind today, thus making them a member of the Netherworld. This ability however was present at creation.

In order to get a proper understanding of shape shifting, it is important to understand the laws and principles of creation. It is also important to understand the condition of man in his first estate and what it was man lost through the act of sin. When man was first created he possessed 100% use of his brain. His intellect was perfectly joined with his physical and spiritual abilities. He was in tune with all nature and creation. Telepathy, empathy, and many other psychic abilities that we believe to be rare and supernatural were an everyday part of his natural estate. Psychic abilities were to Adam and Eve a part of life just as eating and breathing are for us today. This was because Adam and Eve were complete. When God created them they were like a hard drive with all the software already downloaded and installed. God had given them every skill and ability they needed in order to fulfill His command to rule over all of creation.[2] One skill they were given for this authoritative position was the ability to communicate with every aspect of creation in order to control it. Let me give you an example.

Adam and Eve had the ability to communicate telepathically with any creature in its own language. Add to that the fact that every creature loved then in such a way that its desire was to do their will. It was not until after sin entered the world that God placed the fear of man on every

---

[2] Genesis 1:26-28: The word dominion is the Hebrew word *raw-daw* meaning to rule over. Ruling involves controlling, governing, moderating, restraining and managing with direct influence as counsel and guide.

living creature.[3] Prior to that man had a wonderful relationship with every plant and animal on the planet. He was the representative of God to them. There was no death, pain or sickness and there was no animosity, apprehension or fear to muddle the relationship. Everyone and everything was in perfect harmony. Adam and Eve could call upon any creature for any task and it would obey immediately and effortlessly. For instance, Adam and Eve might ask a whale to come to them and to tell them about various areas of the oceanic floor or how the plankton levels were in the area. This direct communication with the creatures was a part of the job God had committed them to doing. It was only the tip of the iceberg in what they could do. Man's complete potential is staggering! God said that whatever man could conceive he could accomplish.[4]

A second *supernatural ability* Adam and Eve possessed was to be able to see the spiritual realm. They could clearly see angels and a part of their daily routine was to associate with the angelic host. Today, people get terrified or overly excited if they get touched by the supernatural. For Adam and Eve it was a normal and necessary part of their day.

---

[3] Genesis 3:17-19, 9:1-7 Man did not even eat meat until after the flood.
[4] Genesis 11:6

We must remember at this period in time that man was in a state of innocence. There was no fear of angels or monsters. Prior to the fall of man fear did not exist. Everything was created good and existed in a state of peace and harmony.[5]

In summation when man was created God had equipped him with every possible ability and trait. During this time period he openly walked with God and commonly spoke with plants, animals and angels.[6] This was a necessary function that Adam needed to be able to do in order to rule over creation. In the next section I would like to show from the Scriptures the part angels play in regulating nature. I would like to expound on the *power of angels.*

---

[5] Genesis 1:31
[6] Genesis 3:1-5: The serpent spoken of here is "The Old Serpent," which is another name for the devil a fallen angel created by God. See Revelations 12:9 for reference.

"And I saw another mighty angel come down from heaven, clothed with a cloud: and a rainbow was upon his head, and his face was as it were the sun, and his feet as pillars of fire: And he had in his hand a little book open: and he set his right foot upon the sea, and his left foot on the earth, And cried with a loud voice, as when a lion roareth: and when he had cried, seven thunders uttered their voices. And the angel which I saw stand upon the sea and upon the earth lifted up his hand to heaven, And sware by him that liveth forever and ever, who created heaven, and the things that therein are, and the earth, and the things that therein are, and the sea, and the things which are therein, that there should be time no longer."[7]

What an awesome picture is painted by the writer of Revelation on the magnitude and power that some angels possess. Angels are incredibly powerful entities with almost limitless abilities. From the Scripture above, we see that angels are the servants of the living God. Angels are God's ministering spirits created to regulate and control all the various intricacies of the universe.[8] This concept of

---

[7] Revelation 10:1-3, 5-6

[8] Hebrews 1:7, 14: Verse 7 informs us that angels come in a variety of forms that include earth, wind, fire, rain, ice, etc. In verse 14 we learn

7

angelic forces being used in the natural world is nothing new. It is a fundamental belief shared by every religion of the world,[9] whether it be Druids, Bards, Animists, Wiccans, Necromancers, American Indians or any culture no matter how advanced or primitive it is. All share one common, ancient belief in the existence of both good and evil spirits and their ability to influence the natural world. The Holy Bible teaches about the position of angels in influencing the physical and spiritual realm of man. For instance every culture of the world has beliefs of the battle between good and evil. In Christianity the belief is that there are three combined forces of evil working against the good will of God. These three forces are:

1) A person's flesh

   a. It is no secret that our bodies often crave things that will impact it negatively, even in many cases shortening a person's life.

   b. The natural inclination of the flesh is to shy away from exercise or hard work but physical exertion is a necessary function needed to keep a body strong.

that the angels are ministering spirits to those who are the heirs of salvation. God uses angels in the function of the tangible creation.
[9] Even deists believe that spirits are active in the world.

2) The body will crave foods that are saturated with sugars and fats which are destructive to the body as anyone in medicine understands; the body will shut down and die from gross obesity. It is a form of suicide. There was a period in my life where I was a 130 pounds overweight, my doctor told me I was eating myself to death. He said, "Tom you are digging your own grave with a spoon, you need to put a hole in that spoon or you are going to die!"

3) The world:

   a. The world system and views are openly opposed to that which lifts up God and seeks to emanate His will with an obedient spirit.

   b. The world seeks its own way trying to forget the God that created it, seeking to worship and serve the creation rather than God.[10]

4) The Devil:

   a. The devil is the head of the array of fallen angelic forces that were cast down from heaven for following the

---

[10] Romans 1

rebellion of the head angel Lucifer, who wanted to be like the true God.

b. They now work in opposition to all of the will of God seeking to destroy all that is good and wholesome to life and liberty.

c. They are completely dark and negative sucking the life from everything they influence.

d. They are devious and diabolical continually scheming in how they can control, possess and destroy man, who is made in the image of God.

e. This battle of good and evil happens between the obedient angels of God that work to carry out the will of God in His creation. The evil angels seek to destroy the works of God and to hinder His word's promises to his children and his decreed will from being carried out upon earth. When it enters the human realm it is identified as being spiritual warfare because it is fallen angels seeking to control and influence the person's spirit for destruction.

The Bible tells us that the *spirit of* sin will seek to have control over us but that we will have the ability to choose to either give it ground to enter us or we can reject it and not give it entrance into us. We have the ability to rule over it.[11] The devils seek to deceive man; they bring the spirit of fear with them to open doorways for gaining ground into an individual.[12] Fallen angels continually seek to enter into men and woman in order to inhabit them and if possible to possess them.[13] This is a main reason for spiritual warfare. Ephesians chapter six describes the angels involved in the war for the spirit.

"Finally, my brethren, be strong in the Lord, and in the power of his might. Put on the whole armour of God, that ye may be able to stand against the wiles of the devil. For we wrestle not against flesh and blood, but against principalities, against powers, against the rulers of the darkness of this world, against spiritual wickedness in high places. Wherefore

---

[11] Genesis 4:7
[12] Deuteronomy 11:16; 2 Thessalonians 2:10; 2 Timothy 1:7; Ephesians 4:26-30
[13] Genesis 4; Matthew 16:23; Mark 8:33; Luke 4:8, 8:30; John 13:27

take unto you the whole armour of God, that ye may be able to withstand in the evil day, and having done all, to stand. "[14]

The titles of the angel's positions depict their abilities and the sphere of their influence. The angelic kingdom has a hierarchy that is very well structured and orchestrated. Though they compose a kingdom of chaos, cooperatively they function with a rigid set of rules placed in order by those holding authoritative positions over them. Like a well equipped militant operation they strive for an overall agenda waiting for the last and final battle of good versus evil. The final showdown where Lucifer, Satan the devil and all their minions and followers will be defeated by the Lord Jesus Christ and His angelic armies before being cast into the lake of fire for all eternity.[15] The following is a list of the angelic hierarchy:

1) Principalities:[16]

    a. A principality is an entity that has pre-eminence, rule, and authority over all the other angels in his area of influence.[17]

---

[14] Ephesians 6:10-13

[15] Revelations 19-22

[16] Jeremiah 13:18; Romans 8:38; Ephesians 1:21,3:10, 6:12; Colossians 1:16, 2:10, 2:15; Titus 3:1

[17] Daniel 10:13,20-21, 12:1; Matthew 9:34, 12:24, 20:25; John 12:31,14:30, 16:11; 1 Corinthians 2:6,8; Ephesians 2:2

b. Principalities rule over terrestrial regions of the earth commanding all the angels in their area. They often will inhabit the person who has the most influence in that area, using it as a throne from which they will rule. An example of a principality is found in Daniel chapter ten. In this account a powerful angelic messenger has been sent from the true God to answer the prayers of Daniel but the principality of Persia had withstood the angelic messenger for twenty one days until God sent Michael, a arch angel to help his messenger get to Daniel. After delivering the message the angel tells Daniel that he must return to fight with the principality of Persia and that the principality of Greece would next come to contend with Daniel.[18] In this account we see the war between God's angels of light against the satanic principalities of darkness.

---

[18] Daniel 10:10-20

2) Powers:[19]

    a. Powers are spirits that have authority over:

        i. Individuals, specifically those in powerful positions or positions of influence. They also take position of power of influence over family lines, claiming authority over the children and children's-children continuing their rule for sometimes thousands of generations until the spirit of sin and the generational curses are destroyed.

        ii. Over regions: Powers can place coverings of darkness and evil over areas that have been dedicated to them through formal ceremony, acts of worship, or heathen, idolatrous practices. Also areas of land where great evil has happened are given invitation and authority for a

---

[19] Ephesians 6:12

Power to establish a dark covering where it will work from to increase its area of influence by spreading out its cloak of darkness. Over the centuries many writers have written of darkness that comes upon the land where a great evil has happened. The darkness then spreads from that point, killing everything good, leaving the land desolate, filled with thorns and briers and often dry. This covering of evil can spread, covering vast amounts of land, even whole regions.[20]

iii. Businesses: Some businesses are of particular interest to the kingdom of darkness for the purpose of extending their demonic reign of influence. Often these businesses will be

---

[20] Psalm 44:19; Isaiah 34:13, 35:7 (for a reversal of the cursed land); Jeremiah 9:11, 10:22, 49:33, 51:37; Malachi 1:3

considered the most philanthropic or just in their causes for humanity. They often will be generous in giving to the needy or causes of good. This is because they seek to create unholy alliances by the means of unequally yoking themselves to the unwary. This unholy union gives them authority to influence the decision making abilities of all those associated with the business. This is just one of the many ways a business comes under the influence of a king of darkness. A *Power* will enter into an agreement with those who have authority over the business. Those on the receiving end of the agreement rarely know they have been brought into a relationship with a king of darkness. By choosing a philosophy of conduct that goes against the revealed will of the true God the persons business is automatically placed under the authority of the kingdom of darkness. The power will place its covering over the person's mind and heart and will then begin to spread a veil of darkness over the entire business. The dark covering of the business will taint and affect every person and business that it comes in contact with it. This is the reason that the Bible teaches that we are to offer everything to the true God in prayer, giving Him praise for it and then to ask for the true God's blessing upon the items we buy.[21] The owners of the business do not have to have to do an actual ceremony[22]

---

[21] Job 34:4; Romans 14:14; 2 Corinthians 6:14-18; 1 Thessalonians 5:18; 1 Timothy 4:3-4

[22] Some businesses are intentionally given over to the kingdom of darkness. I have worked with 100's of occultists who have given me vivid descriptions of the preparations they have gone through in order to prepare for lavish ceremonies of demonic empowering and

or engage in an actual agreement acknowledging the power or the kingdom of darkness for this to happen. It can be done in ignorance of spiritual laws by simply giving themselves over to practices that honor the kingdom of darkness. All that needs to take place, for the Power to establish its position of authority is for the owners, or those in positions of authority in the business, is to give themselves over to the leading of a devil. Let me state this clearly: By rejecting God's holy principles and standards declared in the Bible as the guideline and practice of the business the business is automatically given over to

---

dedication to specific entities in order to have the power and influence of a prince of darkness in their business. These ceremonies specifically seek to influence all they touch.

witchcraft through default.[23]
Many business practices that violate God's word are considered ethically and morally right in societal practice. No matter how philosophically right something may appear to be, if it contradicts the word of God, than it is of the kingdom of darkness, and for this cause, a Power has the right to rule over it. On the other hand if a business intentionally is given over to the true God and sets its order of practice according to God's revealed word it will have the protective hand of God upon it with His Holy Spirit leading and guiding those involved. It will

---

[23] Witchcraft is choosing your own way over God's revealed will. It is the sin of rebellion. Rebellion, though often subtle gives a power authority over the business.

also become a source of influence to all that it touches.[24]

iv. A power is a powerful devil that has the ability to place a dark covering over someone or something. This authority will influence all of the decision making abilities for the kingdom of darkness.[25] They will manipulate thoughts, emotions and actions. This is illustrated in the veil covering the head of a married woman. It was a symbolic gesture showing that she was married and under the authority of her husband.[26] It was a sign of respect for her husband telling others that he was her spokesperson in the

---

[24] Psalm 34:7; Matthew 6:13; Luke 11:4; Romans 15:7; 1 Corinthians 10:31; 2 Corinthians 4:15

[25] There are good, elect angels that watch over God's children allowing for the power of the Holy Spirit to lead, influence and guide in a way that honors God and brings Him glory.

[26] I Corinthians 11:10

congregation.[27] If the woman is not married than she would be under the authority of her father while he was living and if he passed away she would go under the authority of the eldest son. When an angelic entity places its dark veil over its subject, it symbolizes its power and authority over the individual. As previously stated the dark covering can be over a person, family line, territory or business.

3) There are three Hebrew words for devil. One that is used in the Scriptures is the word "*shed*." This is where we get the term shade from.[28] The word shade literally means that which tries to intercept the rays of the sun in order to keep the person from receiving the light of the Sun. It is a dark covering. When the Bible uses the word shed for devil it is describing the purpose of the

---

[27] I Corinthians 14:34; 1 Timothy 2:12
[28] Deuteronomy 32:17; Psalm 106:37

shade. The shade is a creature whose sole design is to stand between God and his people in order to keep them from worshipping God and receiving the blessings from God and the power that God has for their life. The shade is a creature of the darkness and when it is assigned to a person it becomes a dark covering over them, covering them with the power of the kingdom of darkness, which is void of all light. I have worked with many individuals coming out of the occult and they have told me how they will actually do rituals to summon and place shades over the children and children's-children so they will never be able to hear the truth of salvation. In essence they seek to condemn their children to service to the kingdom of darkness. Jesus Christ is the light of the world, the darkness cannot take him in, the shade can only *try* to stand between you and your God. The shade can only try to sever you from the power of God in your life.[29] The only way the shade can accomplish this is by trying to take your eyes off of God and to place them

---

[29] John 8:12, 1:5: Isaiah 59:1-3; Romans 1:28

on anything but the true Lord Jesus Christ. If he can do this he will next seek to lead you into sin, further separating you from the convicting power of God. They do this so they can create a demonic stronghold in your life.[30] This is spiritual warfare! A stronghold is when a person feels helpless and hopeless to be free from a particular sin, circumstance or situation they are in. Jesus is the hope of the world.[31] The shade cannot create a stronghold in a person as long as they hold to this truth!

4) Rulers of the darkness of this world

    a. Rulers of darkness are literally: *Kosmokrator skotos*: meaning that there are a group of angels that are rulers over the darkness of this world. The darkness of this world speaks of the practices, places and inhabitants that are separated from the light of Jesus Christ. These Rulers oversee the Powers that are the coverings spoken of previously. The rulers of darkness dictate, govern and

---

[30] 1 John 2:16; James 1:14; Ephesians 4:26-27; 2 Corinthians 10:4
[31] Psalm 22:9

formulate the plans on how the kingdom of darkness is to spread its affect and control. The ruler is the angel that knows the bigger picture of Satan's plans and he insures that all under his command are working to bring about the fruition of the greater agenda. The power is under the command of the Ruler.

b. The primary effect of darkness is to separate people, places and items from the influence and power of God's Holy Spirit. They seek to mask the truth of man's position and place, in the scheme of God. They seek to blind man to the truth of His condition and to hinder His ability to come to the realization that he is in need of salvation.[32] They manipulate and bend the will of the unregenerate with deceit, lies and trickery.[33] The Rulers command where the powers are to concentrate their

---

[32] 1 Corinthians 2:14
[33] Ephesians 2:1-3

efforts in order to spread their dark coverings.

c. One important thing to note is this: Rulers also can take a position over the heart of an individual. When a heart has been shattered and broken, pain, bitterness and hatred open the doorway for a person to be given over to darkness. A Ruler of darkness can work through an individual that has been deeply wounded. If they can establish a dark throne in the person they will use that person to bring about greater schemas of the kingdom of darkness. It would not be uncommon for a Ruler of darkness to work in the hearts and mind of a parent and then the child to bring about their plan for evil. Time is on their side. They work towards the greater goal of the kingdom of darkness.

d. One example of how a Ruler of darkness uses a person's heart from which to work would be in the case of those involved in mind control programming.

The dark throne in the programmer will enable them, to without mercy, guilt or remorse, shatter the minds of small children and infants through trauma based pain and torture. When the abuser shatters the mind, the power of darkness takes authority over the broken shards of the child's psyche placing powers of darkness over each of the splits[34] to keep them separated and enslaved. These dark coverings keep the broken pieces of the child's heart and mind bound in a state of helplessness and hopelessness. They will remain in this state for the duration of their life unless someone that is lead by the Holy Spirit of God takes the time to help them come to healing, cleansing and restoration. The Ruler of darkness ensures that the job of separating the child's mind is complete, placing a dark covering over each of the separate pieces. The heart will be shattered with

---

[34] Splits is the term used for creating alternate personalities as in dissociative identity disorder

coverings of darkness placed over each of the individual shards, keeping the person from ever having a whole heart. This is done to keep the person from ever being able to search for the true God with all of their heart.[35] The plan is to prevent the person from ever obtaining true freedom and deliverance. It is the cruelest and most diabolical form of abuse there is. The person with the ruler of darkness in them will seek to completely enslave the heart, mind, soul and spirit of others giving them lives of pain, hurt, bitterness and hatred for others and the true God. They not only seek to destroy the lives of their victims but they ultimately want them to suffer complete damnation at the end of their lives being cast into hell for all of eternity. The Rulers of darkness work in some of the following ways:

---

[35] Jeremiah 29:13

i. They render people spiritually blind to the things of the true God.[36]

ii. They keep people in ignorance of the divine things of God to include human responsibilities and duties to Him. This results in ungodliness and immorality and will eventually lead to consequent misery in hell.

iii. Rulers take control of a person's thoughts, their mind and their emotions. They seek to bring the person completely under the command of the dark ruler. They do not do this by blatantly evil thoughts rather they slip in and mingle truth, emotion and falsehood. They continue the work until the person is no longer sensitive to the difference between wrong and right. When a person has lost the ability to

---

[36] John 12:40; Romans 11:7; 2 Corinthians 3:14, 4:4; 1 John 2:11

know wrong from right they are called a reprobate by the Bible.[37] These individuals will often be incredibly devoted to a religion or greater cause of good. They are the *beautiful* side of evil. Often they will take part in philanthropically engineered organizations. Money, power, and position are some of the tools they use to further their influence. The world's values of what it is to be successful are very different than what the Bible classifies as success. A person with a ruler of darkness in them will often live a very wholesome and good life. In this way they will have the greatest amount of influence to use for destroying lives and further

---

[37] Jeremiah 6:30; Romans 1:28; 2 Timothy 3:8; Titus 1:16

spreading   the   powers   of
darkness.[38]

5) Spiritual wickedness in high places

    a. Spiritual wickedness is the result of pervasive idolatry. Spiritual Wickedness in High Places is an angelic entity that rules over those that are given over to pervasive idolatry. Churches all over the world are havens of spiritual wickedness! These religious rulers of the heart, enslave and damn entire groups and civilizations. If it were not for the power of God's election none would be saved from their damnable effect. These are very powerful entities that inhabit all false religious leaders. They can be found in Christian pulpits and hidden in cults. They work through the spirit of the person rather than the intellect. Rather than expounding the truth of God's word these leaders under the control of a Spiritually wicked spirit will water down

---

[38] Ephesians 2:1-3

the Word or leave it out altogether. A dear friend brought it to my attention that the mega-churches of today no longer preach the word of God in its entirety; rather they just give the *"cliff note"* version. We need all of the council of God if we are to live a life that is surrendered to God. These entities will tickl your ears and touch your heart with *good spiritual experiences* of praise and worship, all the while leading you into damnation.[39] These angels of spiritual wickedness assign the rulers of darkness over individuals, groups, denominations and organizations which in turn distribute the angelic powers of darkness amongst the members. They work in unison with the principalities over regions but are in rank and position over principalities. I have talked with many Satanists that told me they were assigned to churches in order to infiltrate and destroy it from within. They said they

---

[39] Matthew 7:13; 2 Timothy 2:16, 3:1-9; Jude

31

would feign salvation and then ask to get baptized. This would make them a member of the church. Once they were a member of the church, since they were also a Satanist it would give their entire coven of cultist the authority to curse, hex and vex the members. Spiritual warfare is real and so is the effect of fallen angels.

b. These religious spirits work to draw devotion and worship away from the true God unto themselves.[40] They seek to blind and mislead mankind, keeping them from the truth of God's word and will. They stir up spirits of animosity against God's truth and His word when it is offered in a literal sense. They seek to lead mankind in rebellion against the Lord God and His Christ. This is the core of Lucifarian worship. These spirits seek to dethrone God and to place the throne of Satan or Lucifer in the hearts of men, making them children of the

---

[40] Deuteronomy 16:18-22; Psalm 146:8

beast; i.e. children of the damned.[41] When a person comes under the control of a ruler of spiritual wickedness in high places it is because they have placed themselves under the mark of the beast.[42]

c. These spirits rule over those that refuse to give God control over their hearts, minds, souls and spirits. They are over those that are self- willed.[43]

d. Those under the effect of these entities will trade true devotion and worship, with an adherence to the literal authority of the Scriptures, for a religion that makes them feel sincere and safe. There will be no fear or reverence of the true God nor true fear of condemnation and a literalness of hell to those under the effect of this spirit.

e. You can identify those under the spell of these spirits by clear and evident signs.

---

[41] Isaiah 14; Ezekiel 28; Deuteronomy 6:4-9; Revelations 13:16-17, 14:9,11, 15:2, 16:2, 19:20, **20:4**

[42] Deuteronomy 6:4-9 shows God's mark upon an individual. Revelations 16:2, 19:20

[43] Job 41:31

For instance, they will often equate their devotion to God by their experience of worship; i.e. their feelings and emotions rather than the truths conveyed in the word of God. They have a subjective form of worship; what's in it for me mentality. Does it make me feel good?

f. When I was new in my Christian life I got very excited about the prospects of Pastoring so I approached an individual that I respected and expressed the possibility of being called to a small church. He turned to me and said that he could never consider a church of less than 400 members as he had to have a large salary to support his lifestyle. He was in the ministry for the money, not the calling.

g. These religious entities control churches, denominations and even countries. They are the epitome of the spirit of the anti-christ and as a false-christ[44] they are leading all of their followers into hell.

6) Stars[45]

Note: Stars can manifest themselves in people. They appear as bright lights in the canvas of darkness. These are the ones that expose themselves in the lives of those they inhabit. They make up a large portion of the angels that join themselves, genetically to individuals at conception creating the Nephilim.[46] I have given a listing of the many aspects of Ashtoreth because she is Biblically called the Queen of Heaven. When she is enthroned in the heart of a person she becomes the spiritual embodiment of worship and idolatry. By controlling the lifestyle of the individual from birth to death she is able to influence thousands of individuals. Through these widespread living temples[47] she is able to procure worship and devotion for decades from all that fall under her sinful snares.

---

[44] Anti Christ means a psudo Christ or one just like. The word Christ speaks of the anointed one of God, who could lead and deliver those who follow Him.

[45] Deuteronomy 4:19, 18:10-14, 17:3; 1 Kings 22:19 2 Kings 23:5 10, 24; Nehemiah 9:6; Job 38:7; Psalm 33:6, 148:1-5; Jeremiah 19:13; Zephaniah 1:5;Acts 7:42; Revelation 12:3-4,9

[46] Genesis 6:1-6, (4); Joshua 1:14, 6:2, 8:3, 10:7; 1 Samuel 2:4; 2 Samuel 10:7, etc. There are 72 references in the Scriptures to the gibborum, i.e. mighty men. An hybrid of angelic unity to human flesh.

[47] A living temple is the embodiment of the goddess or god in the person. Sexual acts, violence, or other types of sin are actual forms of idolatry, devotion and worship for the entity.

35

a. In the Bible, the word **stars** is a general term used to describe the host of heaven or the mass of angels in their entirety. It implies a army that is well orchestrated and active. Scripture implies that when angels where created that a star was also made and placed in the heavens as a physical representation of their spiritual being. Just as there is set order in the solar system there is also a direct order to the angelic host.

b. The relation of the stars can be seen in the following illustration. The Sun is the center of our solar system. The earth and other planets all revolve around the sun. Furthermore all life is dependent upon the sun and the earth's relation to the sun. So it is with Jesus Christ. He is the center of all creation and everything is dependent upon him for their life and existence. *"For by him were all things created, that are in heaven, and that are in earth, visible and invisible, whether they be thrones, or dominions, or principalities, or powers: all things were created by him, and for him: And he is before all things, and by him all things consist.*"[48] All the angelic realm and all of creation are dependent upon Christ. All life revolves around the Lord Jesus Christ.

    c. In the kingdom of darkness Lucifer/Baal sits as the false sun with Ashtoreth/Baalite as the moon. One light to work in broad daylight the other to rule over all the others stars of the fallen angelic host.

    d. Some examples of stars would be:

        i. Artemis[49]

"The Diana of the Romans is the goddess Artemis spoken of in the book of acts. ... she was undoubtedly a representative of the same power presiding over conception and birth which was adored in Palestine under the name Ashtoreth. She is therefore related to all the cognate deities

---

[48] Colossians 1:16-17

[49] Acts 19:24, 27-28, 34-35: The name Diana in these verses is actually Artemis in the Greek

of that Asiatic Juno-Venus, and partakers, at least, of their connection with the moon."[50]

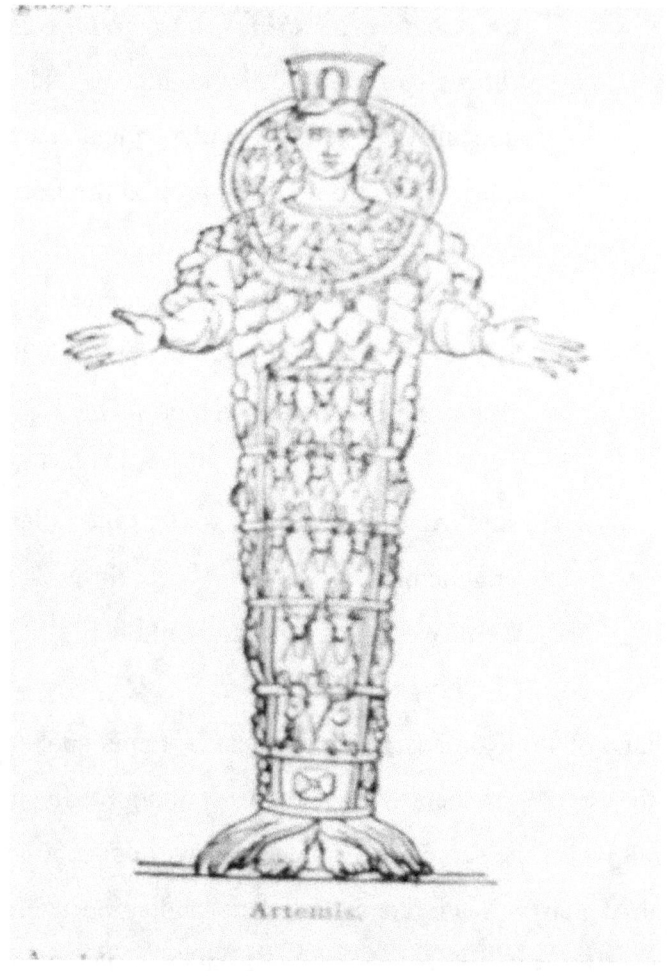

Artemis.

ii. Ashtoreth

A common custom of sexual hospitality is said to have been a practice among people who are otherwise jealous

[50] The Popular and Critical Bible Encyclopedia and Scriptural Dictionary, 1901; Chicago , The Howard-Severance Company

preservers of female chastity. This custom of sexual hospitality was to provide a guest with a female companion, who was usually the wife or daughter of the host. This is believed to have been the custom of Sodom and Gomorra and all the Canaanite regions. It was a practice that spread from Egypt to India in the early ages. This is the reason why it was not strange when Lot offered his daughters to the sexual assaulters in the book of Genesis.[51]

iii. Astarte

Astarte was the Phoenician moon goddess. Her worshippers practiced sacred prostitution and promiscuous intercourse between the sexes during certain religious fetes.

iv. Anaitis

---

[51] Genesis 19

Anaitis is the Armenian moon goddess. In Armenia the children of the middle to upper class families were given by their parents over to the service of Anaitis for sometimes years. The children were reared in the knowledge that it was their duty to gratify the sexual desires of visitors and strangers in service to the deity. The females with the largest number of sexual engagements were the most sought after for marriage. They were believed to be the embodiment of the goddess of love and sexuality.

v. Isis

The worship of Isis is a very strange. On the appearance she is considered to be one of the great goddesses and is associated with being the great mother, wife, a patron over nature and magic and friend of all slaves. The picture painted of her is very positive but what is known but never spoken of openly is that behind the scenes she is also the goddess of prostitution and her priestesses and worshippers are holy prostitutes. Her name in Egyptian means *she is the* throne. What is not commonly known is that the goddess has the ability to merge with other gods and goddesses. In similar form to the worship of Diana the followers of Isis will offer themselves to strangers and visitors to meet their sexual needs. Historian wrote that even as late as the 1800's the worshippers of Isis would line the sides of the river in Bubastes where they would do a dance of enticement to offer themselves to all who would pass by. It did not matter if the taker was man, woman or sought the prostitutes service for their animal, every form of debauchery was offered and practices. As the goddess of nature, magic and sexuality, (sexuality is considered a great part of nature) cats were holy unto the goddess. She was often seen as having a great cat, i.e. a lioness, ocelot, panther or some other form of great cat sitting between her legs as she would stand over it. The female sexuality was seen as that which tied her to her worshippers by merging the power of the cat and nature through the holy prostitute as they would engage in sexual practice to honor the goddess.

vi. Ishtar

Ishtar is a very interesting goddess of Babylonian religion. She is made up in three parts. In her first aspect she is the goddess of the night; the following is a "Rectangular, baked clay relief panel; modeled in relief on the front depicting a nude female figure with tapering feathered wings and talons, standing with her legs together; shown full frontal, wearing a headdress consisting of four pairs of horns topped by a disc; wearing an elaborate necklace and bracelets on each wrist; holding her hands to the level of her shoulders with a rod and ring in each; figure supported by a pair of addorsed lions above a scale-pattern representing mountains or hilly ground, and flanked by a pair of standing owls. Known as the "Burney Relief" or the "Queen of the Night".[52]

NOTE:

This file is made available under the Creative Commons CC0 1.0 Universal Public Domain Dedication.

The person who associated a work with this deed has dedicated the work to the public domain by waiving all of his or her rights to the work worldwide under copyright law, including all related and neighboring rights, to the extent allowed by law. You can copy, modify, distribute and perform the work, even for commercial purposes, all without asking permission.

---

[52] http://en.wikipedia.org/wiki/File:British_Museum_Queen_of_the_Night.jpg

Ishtar as the goddess of the night is often called Lilith, the mother of all monster. It is through her aspect as the goddess of the night that the she possesses her followers. She manifests her deity in them creating an unnatural form of sexual attraction to them. Then by their union in coitus or other sexual acts the stars of heaven, (her children) enter into both of the individuals to take up residence. What is not commonly known is that Ishtar seeks to enslave the male counterpart to the female she has manifested her deity in. It is her desire to enslave them through sexual lust for the purpose of destroying their life. By this it is to be understood she does not seek to take their physical life causing them death but rather she seeks to take and destroy all good things in their life. For this cause she is called the mother of all monsters. She brings about death, misery and destruction. Those in her grip are called the most miserable of people. They hide their hatred, shame and disgust of life behind smiles and false pretense. She is the epitome of the angel of death. She is the great goddess of the kingdom of darkness. She rules over the host of heaven as the leading throne and all of her children are the stars, i.e. the host of heaven. Through her rule she ensures their place among mankind so they can best serve the kingdom of darkness. She works in accordance with the sun-god over the day. They are the greater and lesser lights spoken of in the book of Genesis 1:16. The Biblical Queen Esther that was married to the King Ahasuerus was named after the goddess Ishtar. The name Esther means *"a Star."* Many believe that it implies the planet Venus, which in Greek language is the word Aster. This would make her the equivalent to the Syrian goddess Ashtoreth. But it needs to be remembered that the name Esther is a Persian word showing the second aspect of Ishtar, that being the wife and the mother.

The second aspect of Ishtar is that of the wife and mother. Ahasuerus was the king over the entire earth, he was the physical manifestation of the sun-god and his wife, naturally would be the goddess over the night.[53] When inscriptions and images of Ishtar are found they share a significant trait, they always show the sun behind her and they also show her standing on a lion. The lion is her mount and the sun is her husband that is behind her. She is that which ties the natural world to the world of darkness. Her sexuality is contained in the lioness that she rides. It is in her second aspect as the mother and wife that she wears the instruments of a warrior. She gives her body to create the unnatural union of angel and human. It is a battle that is waged against the natural order of creation. It is not natural for man and angel to be linked but Ishtar gives of herself in

---

[53] All of the elite families of the earth practice this. The earth rulers change just like the constellations do. The closer to earth a constellation is, the greater the influence it exerts over the earth. Astrology accounts for the change of world rulers by the changing of heavenly constellations in their proximity to the earth.

this war to create a genetic stronghold inside the offspring thus ensuring the kingdom of the sun-god, the false god of this world is continued. This is the kingdom of Lucifer, whom she serves with all the host of heaven. Lucifer/Baal/Zeus is the anti-Christ and by placing his children, the host of heaven into mankind at birth he is in essence placing his throne over their heart. As the wife and mother it is her responsibility to ensure that her worship and that of the sun-god are continued through their children. Through the joining together of the sun-god and Ishtar, their children will have a star of heaven seated in them from conception to death. This an angelic spirit passes into them at conception, which is their Nephilim. She battles on behalf of her children to ensure that the kingdom of the false Christ continues to spread. It is just as in the days of Noah, people are marrying and given themselves over in marriage to these false spirits of the world. This was the reason God destroyed the world with a flood and this will be the reason that God once again destroys the world, only this time it will be with a fire and it will be complete. Time will be no more. It is the physical manifestation through the woman that ties the goddess of night-the queen of heaven with the forces of nature and earth creating the sons of God, the Nephilim. Esther is actually the title for her being the Northern Star, the Queen of heaven.

The third aspect of Ishtar is the goddess of the earth. In this aspect she has power over all life and sequentially death when she withholds life. She is the goddess of fertility and the giver of all life to include; human, animal and plant. She rules the spirits of all three kingdoms. In this way she can bless or withhold the blessing of life however she sees fit. She places boundaries upon those who serve her. They make vows and commitments. This is where she gets the authority over her subjects. In the story of how she goes into hell she must leave a piece of her clothing at each of the gates to proceed. Her followers are layered in dark coverings that are gates of enslavement. Seven different layers of dark coverings, each with a different garment to cover the persons, spirit. In order for the person to go free they must renounce each of the seven coverings before they are able to stand naked in truth before the True Lord God over all creation. Only in this manner can they confess with all of their hearts receiving Him as their Lord and Savior. Because of the authority of a vow,[54] her followers are subject to her influence and direct will if they do not stay within the parameters of duty and service they have vowed

---

[54] Ecclesiastes 5:4-6; Matthew 5:34-37; James 5:12

to perform to her. To punish her followers she will withhold her blessings of life, releasing curses upon them and upon everyone they come in contact with.

vii.   Semiramis

Semiramis was the wife of Nimrod who was the first world ruler to make the claim to be the physical incarnation of the sun-god. History describes him to be a giant in stature, (30 plus feet in height), and a mighty hunter among men.[55] It is believed that the myth of the Titans came from the story of Nimrod. In order to procure the worship of all mankind he began hunting down and killing all the other giants. He then sought to establish a place where he could rule from and be worshipped by all of the inhabitants of the earth alongside his wife Semiramis, who claimed to be the moon-goddess. The population of the earth at this point in history was not that great, with all of mankind being concentrated in the region surrounding where Noah and his family exited the ark, upon the mountains of Ararat.[56] He began the building of the tower of Babel as a huge astrology tower from which all the host

---

[55] Genesis 10:7-11; 1 Chronicles 1:10; Micah 5:6
[56] Genesis 8:$

of heaven, i.e. the stars/ angels would be worshipped. He believed that he and his wife Semiramis where the greater and lesser lights placed upon the earth to rule over all of mankind and creation. Since the days of Adam and Eve mankind was waiting for the birth of the Messiah, the One who would restore the kingdom of God amongst men. When Cain was conceived Eve literally said I have conceived the Man from the Lord.[57] Eve believed that Cain was the fulfillment of the prophecy of the One who would destroy the power of the devil over mankind. Cain was not the promised One. Cain slew his brother Abel and then sought to hide it from God. It was from this point on that all of the descendants of Adam and Eve would be taught of the seed of the woman that would destroy the power of sin over mankind.[58] Upon the death of Nimrod, Semiramis claimed this title as the as the Queen of heaven and the Mother of god. The inhabitants began worshipping her as the Queen of heaven. In ancient clay tablets Semiramis is seen as the mother holding the child and is considered to be the original, prototype from which all other goddess came. Since she was the original from the valley of Shinar where the city of Babel was founded when God came down and

---

[57] Genesis 4:1
[58] Genesis 3:15

49

confounded the languages spreading mankind to all the corners of the earth, the worship of Semiramis and her child was taken with those that were scattered. This is why she is the same goddess everywhere. This is why Ashtoreth is called the goddess of a thousand names, she is the same goddess Semiramis and all the others listed. Semiramis was the first. All false religion began in Babylon and it will all end in Babylon when Christ comes to judge the god of this world and to destroy all of his followers.

viii. Bel: The Babylonian moon goddess. She ruled over the night and all the host of heaven were under her command. This is the one of the gods that king Nebuchadnezzar worshipped. His wife would have beent he physical manifestation of this goddess.

ix. Al-Uzza

Al-Uzza is the Arabic version of the goddess. She is the wife of Alla, the sun-god, and all of their children are the stars of heaven. The description of Al-Uzza is very similar with all the others dark goddesses except with one exception;

with Al-Uzza we get a clear definition of the three aspects of the goddess. In her three parts she forms a triad goddess which has three completely different faces and bodies that are all combined into the one. She is the goddess referred to as the Biblical Sheba, who was a consort of King Solomon, the greatest of the Israelite kings.[59] Tradition is that she had an affair with King Solomon which resulted in a child being born unto them both back in her Kingdom of Sheba. The Bible lists the linage of Sheba as coming from Cush, the same line as that of Nimrod.[60]What was different about the land of Sheba was that it had a female ruler as Queen instead of a king. She represented the manifested presence of the goddess Al-Lat.

The first aspect is Al-Uzza. Her name means; *The mighty one, the goddess of the morning star.* In this form she is also called *the strong one.* Al-Uzza is the most revered of the Arab deities. To them she is the goddess of the morning and the evening star. You have probably noticed by this time that many of the Biblical names for the true God have been given to this goddess. She tries to take the place as anti-Christ of the true god by claiming his name and title. It is the utmost in blasphemy. Like all of the others fertility and sexual goddesses she is the embodiment of the planet Venus. Inscriptions of this goddess show her with the north star upon her head as a crown and all of the stars of heaven in her blue clearing of a body. This also is mimicry of the true God.

---

[59] 1 Kings 10
[60] Genesis 1:7, 25:1-4; Psalm 72:10, 15; Isaiah 43:3, 45:4, 60:6; Jeremiah 6:20; Ezekiel 27:20-ff.; Joel 3:8; Matthew 12:42; Luke 11:31

"And they saw the God of Israel: and there was under his feet as it were a paved work of a sapphire stone, and as it were the body of heaven in his clearness."[61]

The only difference between the Biblical description and that of Al-Uzza is that Uzza has a great cat sitting between her feet. Usually it is a spotted leopard but it can be any species of the great cats. This links her to the natural world through her sexuality as the Queen of heaven.

The second aspect is Al-Lat, the Mother whose name simply means *the goddess*.(Al-Lah means the god). Al-Lat is more than just the Mother, she is actually the young girl-the virgin and the mother and the Crone. She is all that encompasses womanhood from birth to death. She is the well of both love and war in humanity. Her sacred animal are the big cats with the Lynx being her most sacred. Her tree is supposedly the original tree of life, being symbolized by the acacia tree. In this aspect she is the goddess of fertility and life. She is the earth goddess that connects the heavens to the earth through her bodily manifestation in her followers. Her female worshippers are holy prostitutes which offer themselves in every way possible. This allows the entry of her children, the stars of heaven to take up their residence within the follower. Her symbol is the crescent moon with the sun resting in the base of the crescent which is upon her head as a crown.

The third aspect is Manat which means the Crone, the *goddess of fate or time*. Manet shows the climax of life; in her hands can be found the

---

[61] Exodus 24:10

harvested wheat and small lump of frankincense. This is to represent how the final harvest is an offering that she gives to her husband the sun-god. In the end everything will be given unto him as an offering. This aspect has long dark hair and a pale, white ashen face. She looks like death. Her worshippers use a black stone to represent her. Her heart is cold and black and as hard as a netherstone. She has no mercy to give. She is void of emotion. She is all that sums up the cold hard facts of life and death. She is over fate and is the goddess of destruction and death. as Her sanctuary was the starting point for several tribes. She is known from Nabatean inscriptions, and tombs were placed under She is the moon. Where Al-Uzza is the star-the queen of heaven, this third aspect is the moon-goddess. She can be seen as the final cup bearer offering the cup of death. She is the Crone goddess-the goddess of Death!

x. Diana

The fertility goddess Diana is one of the best known and beloved of the female deities. There is one peculiar trait of Diana that separated her from every other female deity; she also has three aspects but they are each attached back to back forming a conjoined three circle ring. When this entity indwells a person the face that is pointed to the front will be the presenting aspect. It turns its entire body and face in order to take point position in the host.

In her first person she is the Queen of heaven, Luna, Lucina and also sometimes referred to as Meni-the moon. She is seen as having a crescent moon on the top of her head.

Her second aspect is that which is seen by man upon the earth. She is the physical embodiment of the deity inside of her devoted followers. Their bodies are her temples and they do the work of worship by giving themselves over to all forms of sexual practices. In this form she is seen as either wearing a hunting uniform with a bow in her hand as the great warrior or the many breasted goddess of love and fertility. As the goddess of fertility she is responsible for all life to include insects and plants. She is the fullness of the mother earth.

Her third aspect is that Hecate the goddess of death that rules over hell and is lord over all the souls of the dead. in hell Hecate. In this form she takes on quite a twisted perverted state. She is pictured as having all manner of instruments of torture. She is the punisher/torturer. To her pain is love and love is pain. Life is death and death is life. This aspect has a complete reversal of what is right and godly in life. She seeks to take to hell, all that follow her, so she can punish and torture them for all of eternity.

xi.   The Queen of heaven:

Each of the goddesses share the title, *Queen of heaven*. This is a Hebrew term; *mel-ek' keth hash-shaw-mah'yim* and is the title of the goddess of the moon among the Assyrians from which the roots of the worship of the goddess began. To the children of Shem the Queen of heaven was known as Astarte or Ashtaroth. It for this goddess that cakes were baked, having the image of the moon stamped on them and then presented to her in sacrifice as an act of worship.[62] In Babylon the custom was that every woman born in Babylon was obliged by law, once in her life to submit herself to the embrace of a stranger in order to voluntarily show her worship and submission to the goddess. They would go to the temple and would remain there until they were chosen by a visitor. In the act of worship they would surrender themselves completely to the stranger to be used however they wanted.

xii. Venus

Venus is the Roman goddess of love, fertility, beauty and sex. She is all the embodiment of what is feminine and desirable. Astrologers equate her as being one of the primary gods of worship and influence. Though she may have a place in the solar system and within mans

---

[62] Jeremiah 7:18; 44:17-19, 25

hearts she is nothing in comparison to the true God. The Bible says that God hung that vast expanse of space with a span between his thumb and forefinger. This means Venus is like a speck of dust to Him.[63] He not only created the stars but he gave them their position and their place in the order of creation. Here is some information on the stars and planets.

    e. Each star is but a single part in a larger grouping of stars, which when together create a greater constellation that in turn is a part of a greater galaxy. Some examples would be the constellation of Orion, Taurus, Leo, and Draconian.

    f. Astrology is based upon the belief that each star represents the influence that groups of angels working together have, upon the life of an individual. These constellations supposedly create the mind, intellect and emotions of the person making up their personality. Supposed the constellation group works to control the long-term destiny of

---

[63] Isaiah 40:12: see also Genesis 1:16; Deuteronomy 4:19; Judges 5:20; Job 9:7; Psalm 8:3, 147:4; Isaiah 14:13; Daniel 8:10, 12:3; Mark 13:25; Revelations 8:12, 12:4

mankind. Certainly there is some truth to this. If a person seeks out a star and then submits themselves to its authority than it certainly will give daily guidance and direction for the person to follow. But remember the stars hang in a veil of darkness and being such they work for the kingdom of darkness. They will not do what is best for the person but will seek to control and ultimately condemn the individual. Zodiac groupings will lead a person in choices they make. For instance astrology can guide a person in making choices of who they should marry or other life decisions, but is it wise to leave your fate in the hands of a fallen angel? Specific angels from the constellation/group of stars are assigned to individuals at the time and date of their birth. Astrologers believe these stars/angels have direct influence over them personally and to a lesser extent the earth, animals and plant kingdoms.

Their proportion of influence is in direct relation to their proximity to the earth.

g. The tower of Babel was built in order to communicate with the stars/angels for understanding their influence upon nature and man.[64] It was nothing more than a huge astrology tower, built for the purpose of collective-cooperate worship of angels. This is sin, rebellion and idolatry!

h. The worship of stars/astrology is condemned by the Holy Bible in Deuteronomy, Jeremiah and Zephaniah because it is considered demonic worship.

i. An example of the effect of a grouping of stars inhabiting an individual is found in the demoniac of the gadereenes.[65]

7) Watchers:[66]

a. Watchers are a powerful class of angels that hold the position of watching over

---

[64] Genesis 11
[65] Mark 5:9 Legion speaks of a large company of soldiers, i.e. a segment of the host of heaven.
[66] Daniel 4:13, 17, 23

God's people and province to ensure that His will is carried out and obeyed.

    b. Nebuchadnezzar had judgment brought upon him by the decree of the watchers and the demand of the holy one for failing to recognize God as the One, Who had given him the kingdom of Babylon. He was forwarned by God in a dream but still failed to give God the glory due His name and for this he was punished for a period of seven years.

    c. The kingdom of darkness also has its watchers which seek to enforce, protect and carry out the will and authority of Satan upon the earth.

    d. The watchers are of the highest in rank, power and order of the angelic beings.

8) Holy Ones[67]

    a. The holy ones are a specific group of powerful angels that guard the holiness of God. (God's saints are also called his holy ones in various Scriptures).

---

[67] Psalm 89:6-7; Job 5:1,15:15; Daniel 4:17, 8:13; Zechariah 14:5: from the term *kadoshim* in the Hebrew meaning separated ones, those set apart to God (saints=holy ones)

b. As a part of the ruling class of angels they are endued with the authority and ability to issue God's commands. They work in unison with the watchers to enforce the decrees of God.

c. Satan, as a mimic of the Lord Jesus Christ, has his unholy ones which seek to enforce the carrying out of his rule in the kingdom of darkness. They work with a dark class of watchers. Here is where the battle between light and darkness takes place.

9) Thrones[68]

a. Thrones are a ruling class of angels. They are typified as having four cherub positioned at the four corners of their throne supporting and carrying it where ever the throne wills. They are also surrounded by a large number of seraphim which are under their command.

---

[68] Colossians 1:16

b. The title throne signifies that they have a royal throne that they rule from. This puts them into the ruling class of angels.

c. The Throne sits enthroned over the hearts of kings, princes, dictators and rulers which Satan personally places in positions of power over various kingdoms of the earth.[69] They place their throne over the heart of the individual and sit as a false Christ within them controlling all of their thoughts, emotions and decisions.

10) Dominions [70]

a. Dominions are lesser entities that seek to take possession of individuals. Hence the word dominion, they seek to dominate. They do not often succeed in taking control of the person, but when they do, they create a demonic stronghold which will affect every aspect of the person.[71] It becomes ground given over to the

---

[69] Daniel 7:9; Matthew 4:8-9; Luke 4:5-7; Colossians 1:16; Revelations 2:13, 13:2, 16:10
[70] Colossians 1:16
[71] Ephesians 4:30

devil, affecting the person's emotions and ability to control them. While under the control of a demonic stronghold the individual's ability to make godly decisions will be askew.

b. A person does not always have obvious signs when under the control of a dominion. The dominion will not seek to draw attention to themselves but rather they will create and control a spiritual stronghold to house a variety of other spirits.[72] These spirits will often reveal themselves in regulation issues and compulsive sinful patterns. From inordinate thoughts to extreme emotional mood swings, they will create lives that are very chaotic. When a person feels helpless and hopeless in taking control of something in there life it is a stronghold. Some examples are gluttony, smoking, fear, anxiety, etc. You can identify the spirits in a stronghold by this: Whatever the sin problem is, that

---

[72] Luke 11:17-26; 2 Corinthians 10:4

will be the name of the demonic spirit in the stronghold of the dominion.

c. These entities can only take total control over someone who has given themselves completely over to them in some form of sin or depravity.[73] A curse or cursed object can also allow the entrance of a dominion into a person.

d. Demonic strongholds are the result of an inhabiting dominion. The dominion holds the stronghold, not revealing itself but allowing others sinful spirits to do their work in controlling various aspects of the person.

e. Demonic possession results when they force themselves upon an unwilling person. One example would be the person who was unable to speak because of a demonic possession.[74] The Scriptures have many references to demonic spirits, i.e. fallen angels being cast out of individuals.

---

[73] Isaiah 59:1-3
[74] Matthew 9:33, 10:8, 12:28; Mark 1:34, 39, 3:15, 16:17; Luke 11:20, 13:32

The Bible is very clear on the power and the positions of angels in the created universe. They are a well organized group with a structural hierarchy that seeks to fulfill the agenda of the god of this world.[75] Fallen Angels of the kingdom of darkness seek to manipulate and destroy the lives of all mankind. From influencing the thoughts and emotions of individuals to controlling monarchies and vast empires, angels are very involved in every facet of life. Though their power has limitations they are very powerful beings. Angels even have the ability to transform and manipulate the elements of creation. In Nebuchadnezzar's case, they even transformed him into a beast![76]

In summation everything from the green grass you walk on to the orbit of the farthest reaching galaxy has angels assigned over its function and regulation. Angels are a part of the divine order, which regulate, control, keep and maintain the state of order in the tangible universe. Angels seek to inhabit and manifest themselves in mankind. The source of shape shifting is found in the angel. It is the angel that creates the beast within.

---

[75] 2 Corinthians 4:4; Ephesians 6:11
[76] Daniel 4:25, 32-33

Angels and Elements

There is one final area that I would like to cover before addressing the subject of the shape shifter and that is the correlation between angels and elements. For centuries alchemist and scientist have sought means by which they can change the elemental structure of matter. For instance, because of the abundance of lead and its lack of monetary value, alchemists for centuries have sought a means to change lead into gold. What was once thought to be impossible has been become the possible. Science has found that they can change the molecular structure of materials by particle acceleration. They have turned lead into gold. The reason why they haven't capitalized on this knowledge is that they found that the cost to turn lead into gold exceeds the value of the resulting gold. But think of this; by speeding up the particles of the atom you can change the atom into another substance. Angels have this ability.

Through science man has achieved that which was formerly thought impossible, the ability to change the elemental structure of matter. What takes a great deal of effort for man to achieve is a natural talent or the angel.

Angels were the instrument that Adam used to regulate and control life upon the earth. Angels are creatures that can control matter. They work within the fabric of creation. It is nothing for an angel to transform the proton count of an elemental particle, so why should it be any great feat for them to be able to transform the physical structure of a person's body? I propose to you that from the smallest atomic particle in the human body to the light of the largest star in the galaxy, angels are an active influence for maintenance and regulation.

Angels are much more involved in everything around us than we are aware. They are not designed to sleep nor slumber but keep an active role in their position. For instance when discussing the natural elements and the innate ability that angels possess to control them; i.e. earth, air/ wind, water and fire, it is important to understand that they can do much more than just create these elements. If given authority by God, they can use them in devastating ways. All you have to do is take a serious and long look at the aftermath of a hurricane, flood or earthquake to realize how much power can be released in the matter of a few moments and how many lives will be forever changed as a result of the catastrophic outbreak. History records entire civilizations that have been wiped clean by just a single act of nature![77]

a) Earthquakes
    a. Damghan, Iran: 856 A.D-200,000 killed
    b. Antioch and Syria: 526 A.D.-250,000 killed
b) Volcanic Eruption: Mount Vesuvius-Pompey, 79 A.D. Entire civilization killed
c) Tsunamis:
    a. Crete; the Minoan civilization was wiped out 1600 B.C., cir., by a Tsunami caused by a volcanic eruption in Santorin, Greece.
    b. Helike, Greece; in 375 B.C. completely destroyed by a Tsunami. This is the city that is thought to inspiration for Plato's writings of Atlantis.
    c. Alexandria, Eastern Mediterranean was completely destroyed in 365 A.D. by a Tsunami. The force that hit the city was so great that ships were hurled over two miles inland. Thousands were immediately killed.
d) Hurricanes; Tornados; Fires; Floods; Land Slides; etc.

---

e) In the Bible God used angels to do the following:

    a.   One death angel passed through Egypt and killed all of the first born of both man and beast. Any first born person or animal that was not under the protective blood of the sacrificial lamb was killed by the angel of death.[78]

    b.   In judgment for the sin of David, the king of Israel, God sent an angel to slay the people. Only the offering by the King at the threshing floor of Aruanah stopped the death angels hand but still 70,000 men died.[79]

    c.   During the days of Isaiah Sennacherib the King of Assyria came up against Israel. King Hezekiah poured out his heart to the Lord God and in defense of Israel, for King David's sake defended Israel. In one night he sent a death angel that took the lives of the entire Assyrian army; 185,000 soldiers died in the night. The only one left was the king who fled back to his own country where his two sons then murdered him.[80]

---

[78] Exodus 12:12, 29-31
[79] 2 Samuel 24:15
[80] 2 Kings 19:35, 37

The amount of damage and deaths that have occurred from natural events is a subject that can be studied on its own but the general idea is this; the elements contain incredible amounts of energy that can be used to better mankind or to destroy mankind.[81] Angels control he elements and at God's direction, His judgment can be poured out upon mankind. It is at this point where I would like qualify the term *element* with the following definition:

> Elements are simple substances such as wind, fire, water, and earth but on a deeper level they can include natural occurrences such as earthquakes, tornadoes, floods, fires and hurricanes. They also include the natural habitat for instance water is the natural habitat of fishes. In their simplest form they are the chemical elements of matter which singly or in combination compose substances of all kinds. They are the building blocks of all matter.

This is where the nature of the angel lies; it's in their ability to work matter. They are designed to change, manipulate

---

[81] Think of the power of the atomic bomb, neutron bomb, hydrogen bomb or other device of mass destruction.

and even transform the elements of nature. It is this supernatural design that gives them the ability to change a man into a beast. They do it by assimilating themselves into the body of the individual creating a hybrid. The following are potential hybrids.

1) The meshing together of two spirits
   a. Two Human: When it is two human spirits it is called a *twinning*. They take some of the spirit from each person and place inside the other, creating a spiritual tie between the two so they mutually share in each other's life.
   b. Animal and human spirit: This is a hybrid where the angel takes and unites the human and animal spirit enabling them to draw from one another in a symbiotic form of union. The bond is always there below the surface in an unholy tie. A person that has mastered the ability to project their spirit is someone that can project their spirit into that of an animal whenever they choose to. This allows them to experience life for a time through the body of the animal. When the

spirit of the animal is brought into the human the person can draw the animal completely into themselves allowing the animal to have the dominate role. This is a form of allowable possession. The person takes on all of the aspects of the animal.

c. Angel and human:

      i. The Nephilim: If this union begins at conception than it is called a nephilim, a mutual sharing of life between the angel and the human. As the person ages they develop the enhancement of their natural abilities above that which is commonly held by their peers. The angel will give them superior abilities and strengths. They may even have innate abilities that are unnatural or supernatural.

     ii. The Dominion: When a entity enters the person some point after conception they will create a stronghold within the person. When they have done this they will have become a part of the person's thinking patterns and lifestyle choices. If the person has values that oppose those of the entity there will be a great deal of internal stress affecting the person both mentally and emotionally. It is not uncommon for the entity, in an effort to gain greater control over the person, to take control of their health in some way.

iii. Demonic Possession: If the entity is of a ranking or ruling class, such as a star, it will have a group of angels under its authority. If too many entities take up residency within the person the result will be a demonic possession. Demonic possession has varying degrees from emotional outbreaks, bi-polar, to complete loss of mind and control over one's body.

The various forms of anthropomorphism will be discussed in detail in the following chapters. In the meantime let me give you this simple definition:

Therianthropic is the "combining human and animal form, as the centaur; also pertaining to religions in which deities of such forms are worshipped."[82] Theriomorphic is when the person completely takes on the form of an animal.

Before proceeding into this subject I would like to take a sometime to discuss how angels control the elements.

---

[82] Webster's New Collegiate Dictionary; Copyright 1956 by G&C. Merriam Co. Philippines

Angels controlling the elements, wind and water

"And the same day, when the even was come, he saith unto them, Let us pass over unto the other side. And when they had sent away the multitude, they took him even as he was in the ship. And there were also with him other little ships. And there arose a great storm of wind, and the waves beat into the ship, so that it was now full. And he was in the hinder part of the ship, asleep on a pillow: and they awake him, and say unto him, Master, carest thou not that we perish? And he arose, and rebuked the wind, and said unto the sea, Peace, be still. And the wind ceased, and there was a great calm. And he said unto them, Why are ye so fearful? how is it that ye have no faith? And they feared exceedingly, and said one to another, What manner of man is this, that even the wind and the sea obey him?"[83]

Let me preface this account with the following statement: These disciples were seasoned fishermen having been raised on the sea. They were probably more at home on the waters than they were on the land. Until meeting Christ, fishing had been the only life they had known. Facing fierce storms would have been something that they were trained and experienced in dealing with so when reading this account it becomes blatantly clear, this was no

---

[83] Mark 4:35-41; Also found in Luke chapter 8

74

ordinary storm! When this storm came, it brought with it a spirit of fear and death.[84] The disciples were in a state of panic for their lives. Taken in the moment of desperation they ran to the Lord who was sound asleep at the end of the boat and waking him they shouted, "Don't you care that we are going to die?[85]" Christ, rather than shouting out orders to bail harder, rises to his feet and gives the command;

"Peace be still."

The result was immediate. The storm instantly ceased. How could this happen? Naturally speaking, someone shouting at the wind and waves would have no effect upon the storm or their condition. But at the words of Christ everything instantly changed, the winds vanished, the sea was calm and the sun was shining. How could this be? The answer is quite simple; the Lord was not speaking to the storm. He was speaking to one of his created angels.[86] When Jesus spoke those words he was commanding a demonic entity to stop what it was doing. In the literal Greek language what he said was;

"Be muzzled."

Jesus spoke to this demonic spirit in the same manner that a kennel master speaks to one of his trained dogs and the

---

[84] 2 Timothy 1:7
[85] English paraphrase of "Master, carest thou not that we perish?"
[86] Psalm 148:5; Colossians 1:16; Revelations 4:11

75

demonic entity immediately obeyed. Peace was on the water. To put it in plain language; an evil angel was attempting to kill Christ and his disciples and the means he was using were the natural elements of wind and water.

The above example shows how angels can exercise power with the elements using them as a destructive force but in Revelations 7:1, we are given an example of how angels can do just the opposite. Rather than releasing the forces of nature they use their influence in a great feat of restraint.

"And after these things I saw four angels standing on the four corners of the earth, holding the four winds of the earth, that the wind should not blow on the earth, nor on the sea, nor on any tree."

Don't pass this verse by too quickly. At first glance it may seem like no big deal, so the wind doesn't blow for a bit but that is not the case; they stopped all wind movement on the entire earth! It only took four angels to completely stop all air movement upon the entire earth. The implications are quite severe. No wind generated turbines would work; no sailing dependent upon the wind would move; eagles could not fly, aircraft would drop and all life would slowly die and cease to exist. Literally what is being implied is that the four angels made every molecule of air stay right where it was. Your lungs would have to work very hard just for you to breathe.

Friends think about it; the amount of energy that it would take to suppress and hold all of the winds of the entire world is unimaginable but yet here is an example of how in the near future, only four of God's angels will accomplish just that.

Now I would like to show you how angels can change the very fabric of nature, imbibing the inanimate and lifeless with mobility and life.

"And the LORD spake unto Moses and unto Aaron, saying, When Pharaoh shall speak unto you, saying, Shew a miracle for you: then thou shalt say unto Aaron, Take thy rod, and cast it before Pharaoh, and it shall become a serpent. And Moses and Aaron went in unto Pharaoh, and they did so as the LORD had commanded: and Aaron cast down his rod before Pharaoh, and before his servants, and it became a serpent. Then Pharaoh also called the wise men and the sorcerer's: now the magicians of Egypt, they also did in like manner with their

enchantments. For they cast down every man his rod, and they became serpents: but Aaron's rod swallowed up their rods.[87]

In this passage we find an incredible display of the power of transformation. In Exodus 4:3 the Lord has Moses cast his rod/staff down and much to the amazement of Moses, when the staff hits the ground it immediately is transformed into a serpent. It would appear that the staff did not become just any serpent but most likely it was transformed into a poisonous serpent since Moses runs from it. The Lord then tells Moses to reach down and to pick up the serpent and after Moses picks the snake up, while it is in his it turns back into a wooden staff.

We next read in Exodus 7:9 that this time the Lord tells Moses to tell Aaron to cast down his rod and this time it will become a devouring dragon.[88] At the direction of Moses Aaron casts down his staff in front of Pharaoh and Pharaoh has his sorcerers and magicians all cast their staffs down and they all become *tanniyn*.[89] The passage says that the sorcerers and magicians of Egypt were able to

---

[87] Exodus 7:8-12

[88] Dragon means a lizard that preys on others, like a komoto dragon.

[89] In Ex. 4:3 the rod became a *nachash* meaning a serpent but in Ex. 7:10-12 all of the rods become *tanniym* which is the word for devouring dragon.

transform their staff through the use of enchantments. The word used in the Hebrew for enchantments is the word *lah'hat* and it means *a flaming sword* or an *angelic sword.* This is an incredible revelation. The staff of Moses was transformed by the power of God but the sorcerer's and magicians transformed their through the power of an angel. The word enchantment means that through whispering an incantation the spirit was summoned and petitioned to transform the inanimate, lifeless staff into a living creature of flesh and blood. The power to do this was by a very powerful angel. It is believed that each of the ten primary gods of Egypt were present at this meeting, being manifested in the bodies of their sorcerer priests and magicians. When they did their enchantment what actually happened was the angelic host entered into the staff, transforming the actual elemental structure of the staff, changing it into a living, breathing, devouring dragon. These dragons were different than serpents in that they are likened to dragons of the sea. This must have been an incredible display of power but to show the sovereignty of God over all the angelic forces, the dragon that was the staff of Moses attacks and swallows all of the dragons created from the Egyptian staffs. The text suggests that they dragons actually did battle with the staff of Moses being the victor. The rod of Moses in this instance is the prototype of the brazen serpent that would be lifted up giving healing and life to those who were bitten by the fiery serpents as a punishment for their sin.[90] This was an picture of the saving power of the Lord Jesus Christ who would die upon a cross to heal and cleanse us from our sins if we would only look to him as our Savior. The true God can defeat the gods of this world and can cleanse us from every sin; we need to only look to Jesus in order to live.

The battle in Pharaohs court is an example of how angels can change the very fabric of structure while also giving it life. Realize that animals have spirits, but not souls. That is the difference between animals and men. Angels can impart their spirit into an object, changing its atomic structure and imparting their life unto the object but they do not possess a soul, so they cannot give it eternal life. God is the One that gave man life when He breathed into nostrils of Adam and only God can give eternal life.[91]

The next example I would like to show you is from the Book of Daniel, where at the command of an angel, a man is transformed into a hybrid of animal, human and angel.

---

[90] Numbers 21:6-9; John 3:14, 8:28, 12:32-33
[91] Genesis 2:7; 1 Corinthians 15:45;

Angels transforming a man into a beast

"The king spake, and said, Is not this great Babylon, that I have built for the house of the kingdom by the might of my power, and for the honour of my majesty? While the word was in the king's mouth, there fell a voice from heaven, saying, O king Nebuchadnezzar, to thee it is spoken; The kingdom is departed from thee. And they shall drive thee from men, and thy dwelling shall be with the beasts of the field: they shall make thee to eat grass as oxen, and seven times shall pass over thee, until thou know that the most High ruleth in the kingdom of men, and giveth it to whomsoever he will. The same hour was the thing fulfilled upon Nebuchadnezzar: and he was driven from men, and did eat grass as oxen, and his body was wet with the dew of heaven, till his hairs were grown like eagles' feathers, and his nails like birds' claws. And at the end of the days I Nebuchadnezzar lifted up mine eyes unto heaven, and mine understanding returned unto me, and I blessed the most High, and I praised and honoured him that liveth for ever, whose dominion is an everlasting dominion, and his kingdom is from generation to generation:"[92]

I have noticed over the years that when skeptics read something from the Bible that seems supernatural they are quick to discount it as myth or fantasy. Take the story of

---

[92] Daniel 4:30-34

Jonah being swallowed by a great fish, though it seems impossible that a man could live in the belly of a great fish for several days, history has shown that it is not only possible but has happened many times. There are several recorded accounts of men that have lived through being swallowed by whales. Some have been in the stomach of the whale for days before being rescued. Others had been given up for dead by their comrades, only to be found alive after eviscerating the whale. Science always proves that the Bible is correct.

In addressing this passage from the book of Daniel a person would have to willingly ignore a great deal of factual evidence that supports the truth of the Bible to try and discount it as a myth or fictional story. The Babylonian records from that era and many other writing from historians all agree that the King Nebuchadnezzar had a madness come upon him, possessing him for a period of no less than seven years. The records even note that a group of royal soldiers were assigned to protect the king while he grazed as an ox in the fields of Babylon. Friends you cannot write that in history if it is not real. Nebuchadnezzar even wrote about his madness after God restored his mind. Here are a few examples:

1) "The Greek historian Abydenus wrote in 268 BC that Nebuchadnezzar had been "possessed by some god" and subsequently had disappeared from the scene.

2) A Qumran document, "The Prayer of Nabonidus" makes mention of a king of Babylon as a tree being chopped down and spending seven years in insanity.

3) Scholars have noted that although Nebuchadnezzar's accomplishments have been well documented, there is no record of him doing anything between the years 582 BC and 575 BC."[93]

4) "In obvious reference to the king's unusual malady, Berossus, a Babylonian priest of the third century B.C., records that Nebuchadnezzar, having reigned forty-three years, was suddenly invaded by sickness (Contra Apionem 1:20).

5) According to Megasthenes, who lived form 313-280 B.C., the Chaldeans had told him that Nebuchadnezzar, while on the roof of his palace, having completed his military conquests, "was possessed by some god or other."

6) Eusebius, in his Praeparatio Evanelica (9:41), quotes Abydenus concerning Nebuchadnezzar in his

---

[93] http://www.rondaniel.com/library/27-Daniel/Daniel0401.html

last days "being possessed by some god or other" and who, having uttered a prophecy concerning the coming Persian conqueror, "immediately disappeared."[94]

7) Josephus attributes to the Babylonian Historian, Berosus, a definite reference concerning a strange malady suffered by Nebuchadnezzar before his death[95]

8) "And at the end of the days I Nebuchadnezzar lifted up mine eyes unto heaven, and mine understanding returned unto me, and I blessed the most High, and I praised and honoured him that liveth for ever, whose dominion is an everlasting dominion, and his kingdom is from generation to generation:And all the inhabitants of the earth are reputed as nothing: and he doeth according to his will in the army of heaven, and among the inhabitants of the earth: and none can stay his hand, or say unto him, What doest thou? At the same time my reason returned unto me; and for the glory of my kingdom, mine honour and brightness returned unto me; and my

---

[94] http://www.decodingdaniel.com/daniel4/pride.html; Also "A Commentary on Daniel," Leon Wood, The Zondervan Company, 1973 Grand Rapids Michigan

[95] McGee, J. Vernon; Through the Bible with J. Vernon McGee, Volume 3, p.555Nashville, TN. 1982

counsellors and my lords sought unto me; and I was established in my kingdom, and excellent majesty was added unto me. Now I Nebuchadnezzar praise and extol and honour the King of heaven, all whose works are truth, and his ways judgment: and those that walk in pride he is able to abase."[96] This was written in Aramaic not Hebrew and in the first person.

The transformation that over took Nebuchadnezzar is not unheard of; science has a term for it, Boanthropy. What the king experienced is known as **boanthropy**, a combining of a human and an ox to create a theriomorphic being. Though extremely rare this condition has been medically noted.

The British mental institute had a patient that for five years had lived entirely off of just grass and water. He was in excellent health for the period of madness. He was completely given over to the malady and for the duration of his stay at the facility he was allowed to live as an ox outside on the ground of the hospital.[97] Another case of Boanthropy was recorded in Germany with the exception that the German was a woman instead of a man. It is recorded that the woman was housed at the Wurttember

---

[96] Daniel 4:34-37

[97] Raymond, Harrison, *Introduction to the Old Testament*, pp. 1116-17

Asylum for the insane in Germany. They said that during that time period various forms of lycanthropy had become so common that it had lost its shock and appeal. This woman lived entirely off of grass and water for a period of several years. She possessed neither human traits nor characteristics but was in every way an ox.[98]

In both of the above cases, the patients lived entirely on nothing but grass and water for several years suffering no physical detriments. Actually their bodily constitution was in excellent condition. Their mental condition was one of solemnity and peace within their condition; they lived as an ox. They exhibited all the characteristics of an ox to include an aversion towards man, preferring solitude while grazing on the health facilities lawn. Nebuchadnezzar's experience was similar; the man was completely lost and was consumed by the spirit of the ox. Because of this, for his own protection he was driven from man so he could live out his days in the fields of Babylon munching on grass. You may be asking yourself, how is this possible? How can a person live entirely off of just grass and water while still remaining strong and healthy? The answers are given in this text of Daniel four. I

---

[98] Keil, C.F.& Delitzch, F, *Commentary on the Old Testament in Ten Volumes*, Volume 9, p.159-160; Grand Rapids, Michigan 1991

would like to take the time now to examine Daniel 4:28-37 in a verse by verse exposition.

The Transforming Power

As you may have noticed, I have given a great deal of time to the subject of angels. This was in order to establish the foundation for the subject of shape shifting. I propose to you that angels have incredible power to, not only influence mankind and the elements but they also have the ability to transform living and non-living items. This ability when applied to man has the potential to transform his mind, i.e. his ability to think and perceive thoughts, and also his physical body into that of an animal. Complete control happens when the angel has attached itself to the spirit of the person thus controlling the body, mind and spirit creating a complete transformation. This is how *zoomorphism* occurs.[99] Boanthropy is the ailment that had taken over Nebuchadnezzar but zoomorphisms are actually more common than what is popularly believed.

Zoomorphism is something that is found in every stage of mankind. From the earliest writings and ancient hieroglyphics, to modern day practices, from the beginning

---

[99] "Zoomorphism is the representation of God or of gods in the form, or with the attributes, of the lower animals." Webster, Merrium; "Webster's New Collegiate Dictionary," G&C Merriam Co. Pub. Springfield , Mass., USA.

of mans development to the present day there have always been aspects of zoomorphism present. Zoomorphism is much more than just a mental condition where a person takes on, to a greater or lesser extent, the traits and characteristics of an animal. It extends into the vacuum of man's soul where he seeks to fulfill the innate desire to worship something greater than him. Striving to somehow connecting himself to whatever his conception of deity is. Think about it for a moment, do not many cultures around the world depict their gods in zooamorphicological images? Below are some modern illustrations: (Realize that these entities are seriously worshipped and adored by well educated, cultured individuals. Some of the entities listed below have millions of faithful followers who zealously devote themselves to their god.)

    i.   Genesha: Genesha is an ancient god, going back several millenniums and is worshipped by several religious sects. He is a major god of India, Hinduism and Buddhism alike. He is the lord over the host of heaven. Genesha is pictured as a human-elephant combination. He is one of the most worshipped gods upon the earth today with people in America, India and many other countries paying homage to him with the offering of bananas and other items. He literally has 100's of millions of worshippers at this present time.

ii.   Ra: Ra is the ancient Egyptian solar deity. He is depicted as being a man with a birds head. He is the sun god that manifests himself in Pharaoh and also in his priests. Though several millenniums old, Ra is also a deity with tens of millions present day worshippers.

iii.   The Devil: the Devil is depicted as being a man-goat entity. He is considered to be a great god amongst man with tens of millions of worshippers worldwide. He is the embodiment of the wild goat which cannot be tamed or subjugated but rather chooses to live its life however it desires. The Devil seeks to deceive others as to the nature and consequence of their sins. He seeks to lead his followers into lives of rebellion, which is witchcraft in its purest form, and away from the true Lord and God. Rather than surrendering to the will of God the Devil will lead them to resist and to turn away from the true God and unto the sins and cares of the world and self. There are many that worship the devil without even realizing it. By rejecting the truth of the true God's word they have rebelled and embraced the doctrines of the devil. He is the Adversary of the child of God.[100]

iv. Baphomet is the great horned god over many organizations and worshippers. It is often called the goat of Menendez. Baphomet is a combination of both male and female anatomy with that of a three horned goat. He represents both heaven and hell, the sun and the moon. He is the image associated with the Masonic organization and was found to be among the gods of the Knights Templar of the 14th century. He has been described in writings as early as 1195 AD.

---

[100] Mark 8:18; 1 Corinthians 10:21; 1 Timothy 4:1; Revelations 16:14; 1 Peter 5:8

v.   Satan: Satan appears as the combination of a man and a red bull. Satan is the embodiment and anti-thesis of sacrifice to the living God for the cleansing of sin.[101] Satan in the form of a man/bull chooses to have others sacrifice their lives unto him. He is red because he is the fullness of sin, covered with the blood his own sins and those of his followers. He takes life rather than giving it. His desire is to enslave mankind, not set it free. He does this by tempting man to sin against God so he can then use it against him in God's court. He is the Accuser of the breather.[102]

vi.   The embodiment of the goddess: The embodiment of the goddess is a joining of the four elements, earth, air/wind, water and fire to the individual. The reason it is called the embodiment of the goddess is because it is a joining of spiritual entity, plant, and

---

[101] Numbers 19

[102] 1 Chronicles 12:1; Zechariah 3:1-2; Matthew 4:10, 16:23; Mark 4:15, 8:33; Luke 10:18, 3:26, 22:3, 31; John 13:27 ; Acts 5:3, 26:18; 1 Corinthians 5:5, 7:5; 2 Corinthians 2:11, 11:14, 12:7; 1 Thessalonians 2:8; 2 Thessalonians 2:9 ; 1 Timothy 1:20, 5:15; Revelations 2:9, 13, 3:9, 12:9, 20:2

animal to human spirit. It is listed as a zoomorphism because it falls into the category of listing man as one with nature, as the highest form of natural creation. It takes many forms the most popular being the embodiment of the moon as the moon goddess. The worship of the goddess is one of the oldest religions, if not the oldest in the world. Many try to label it as witchcraft but actually it encompasses much more. Everything from ancient Keltic, Celtic Druidry, to all earthen forms of Pagenism and animism. The goddess is not limited to one type of imagery but is able to project into or to summon into herself all spirits, whether they be animal, plant or elemental. She is considered to be the most powerful of all the entity human relationships and the most widely worshipped.[103]

---

[103] Jeremiah 7:18, 44:17-19, 25; Exodus 34:13; Deuteronomy 7:5, 12:3; Judges 3:7; 1 Kings 14:23, 18:19; 2 Kings 17:10, 18:4, 23:14; 2 Chronicles 14:3, 17:6, 9:3, 24:18, 31:1,3,19, 34:3,7; Isaiah 17:8, 27:9; Jeremiah 7:2; Micah 5:14, (Groves is actually the name Ashera also known as Astarte., Joshua 9:10, 12:4, 13:12, 13:31; Judges 2:13, 20:6; 1 Samuel 7:3-4, 12:10, 31:10; 1 Kings 11:5, 33; 2 Kings 23:13; 1 Chronicles 6:71

From the above examples it's easy to identify how widespread and real the concept of zooamorphilogical beings are, in present day societies and cultures around the world.

Just as there are many different representations of the gods, there are many forms of transformation that can happen within a person. The most common is that which affects the mind and the spirit of the person while allowing them to retain their mental awareness. Though they do not always realize it, the union will affect their ability to make judgments. When a spirit enters into a person though an unholy union, the spirit is called an introject. After the introject[104] enters into a person it will work at directing them towards matters of the dark side. For instance, a person in the martial arts may become obsessed with training. This is because if the spirit can place the person focus on a skill, it can greater control over them. They will give themselves over to the leading influence of the spirit little by little. As the spirit gains ground within the individual it creates opportunities for more spirits to enter into the host until a spiritual stronghold is developed. Here

---

[104] James 1:12-15; 1 Corinthians 6:15-19: A introject is a spirit that enters into a person, uniting with their spirit. It has the ability to affect their emotions, moods and both physical and mental abilities. It will seek to gain control of the individual with the intent to dominate and control their life.

is a simplified flow chart of how a stronghold can be developed.

a) A man sees something that causes him to lust; in other word he has an improper/sinful passion. He is tempted to think about what he is viewing. The man can, either turn away from the temptation and cleanse his thoughts or he can give into the thought giving it more significance.[105]

b) If he gives place to the temptation then the spirit of lust will enter into him.

c) The spirit of lust begins tempting him more and more, slowly gaining more ground in the person until he can create a complete stronghold. A stronghold can be identified by the person feeling helpless and hopeless to break the sinful habit.

d) As the spirit gains more ground the man will become more desensitized to the sin. He will lose the original conviction of sin. It is at this point that the spirit will begin working with other spirits to broaden the power and control over the individual.

e) When the man gave up the ground to the spirit of lust by not fighting against its temptation, he willingly given up to the spirit of lust. It is like a

---

[105] 2 Samuel 11; James 1: 12-15

wrestling match where one combatant wears the other down until they finally concedes. By not resisting the temptation the man has given it the spirit ground to work from.[106]

f) The original spirit will now be joined with another spirit to try and tempt the person into another area of inordinate affection. The spiritual world of darkness will work together to gain control over the thoughts and emotions of the host.

g) This cycle will continue until the person finds that they have lost control in some area of their life. It may be an addiction to pornography, gluttony/over eating, anger/emotional issues, etc. The list of possibilities is exhaustive. When a Christian has a stronghold of legalism they will be blind to their condition. They will be judgmental of others, and will get angry over doctrine and other matters of the Scriptures. Remember the wisdom that comes down from the true God is first of all peaceable, not angry or hateful.[107]

h) When the person has lost control of an area of their life than it is called a spiritual stronghold. A

---

[106] Ephesians 4:26-27
[107] James 1:16-21

dominion will rule over the person through the combination and combined effect of all the spirits. When it is a stronghold of legalism it will be ruled by a religious spirit in high places. They will be void of the power of the love of Christ in their life. Instead they will obsess with doctrine not the salvation of others.

The enjoining of spirits, though mostly unnoticed, is actually a very common experience. For instance:

1) Shamanism is based upon the ability to channel entities, energy and spirits through the Shaman. The trained Shaman can even project his spirit out of his body and into other people or animals. (This also includes Voo-doo, Hoodoo, ancestrial priests, Voo-dun and other similar religions.)

2) Witchcraft is a communing and empowering with spirits and entities.

3) Satanism is a contractual agreement between angelic entities and includes consensual possession for empowerment.

4) Eastern Martial arts and Yoga is the consensual channeling and possession of the body by the spirits

of nature. Many forms of the Martial arts are solely based upon the practitioners' ability to channel and become possessed by the animal entities and other spirits, such as death, etc.

5) Mentalist's are individuals that are indwelt with an entity that enables them to influence and manipulate the decision making ability of others, even being be able to project their will into another person's mind.[108]

6) Astrologists also work within the realm of the spiritual supernatural. "Even if your interest is superficial, perhaps you would think twice if you realized that when you turn to astrology you are actually turning to advice from the ancient gods of a peculiar polytheistic religion. ... Its books are well stocked with reference to planets and stars. But as you look deeper into the texts, you realize it's not the planets you're interpreting, it's the *god's they're named after.* Saturn, for instance, is said to affect people in a constricting, malevolent way. But these are not characteristics of the planet-that's just a big

---

[108] This is also a form of psionics. **Psionics** refers to the practice, study, or psychic ability of using the mind to induce paranormal phenomena. Examples of this include telepathy, telekinesis, and other workings of the outside world through the psyche.

sphere with rings around it-it's the god Saturn from ancient Romany mythology who was revered as a threatening and sinister primeval power."[109]

To show the sequence of how a person can be affected by angelic forces I will now turn to the book of Daniel. This passage contains all of the details of what happens in a complete anthropomorphic transformation.

"All this came upon the king Nebuchadnezzar. At the end of twelve months he walked in the palace of the kingdom of Babylon. The king spake, and said, Is not this great Babylon, that I have built for the house of the kingdom by the might of my power, and for the honour of my majesty? While the word was in the king's mouth, there fell a voice from heaven, saying, O king Nebuchadnezzar, to thee it is spoken; The kingdom is departed from thee. And they shall drive thee from men, and thy dwelling shall be with the beasts of the field: they shall make thee to eat grass as oxen, and seven times shall pass over thee, until thou know that the most High ruleth in the kingdom

[109] Strohmer, Charles, "What Your Horoscope Doesn't Tell You," pg.21, Tyndale House Publishers, Wheaton Illinois 1988

of men, and giveth it to whomsoever he will. The same hour was the thing fulfilled upon Nebuchadnezzar: and he was driven from men, and did eat grass as oxen, and his body was wet with the dew of heaven, till his hairs were grown like eagles' feathers, and his nails like birds' claws. And at the end of the days I Nebuchadnezzar lifted up mine eyes unto heaven, and mine understanding returned unto me, and I blessed the most High, and I praised and honoured him that liveth for ever, whose dominion is an everlasting dominion, and his kingdom is from generation to generation: And all the inhabitants of the earth are reputed as nothing: and he doeth according to his will in the army of heaven, and among the inhabitants of the earth: and none can stay his hand, or say unto him, What doest thou? At the same time my reason returned unto me; and for the glory of my kingdom, mine honour and brightness returned unto me; and my counsellors and my lords sought unto me; and I was established in my kingdom, and excellent majesty was added unto me. Now I Nebuchadnezzar praise and extol and honour the King of heaven, all whose works are truth, and his ways judgment: and those that walk in pride he is able to abase."[110]

Possession-transformation does not just happen . . .

I want you to realize this punishment did not just *happen* to Nebuchadnezzar. He had been given a warning.[111] Nebuchadnezzar was a worshipper of Bel which was the name for the moon goddess. She was the counterpart to Zeus who was considered to be the sun-god and the ruler of the day. Bel, as the moon goddess, was the ruler of the night and the Queen over all the host of heaven. Take a look at this ancient engraving, it shows the Babylonian king as the sun god.[112]

---

[110] Daniel 4:28-37
[111] Daniel 4:1-27
[112] Cyclopedia of Biblical, Theological, And Ecclesiastical Literature; McCilntock and Strong; Volume I, pg. 729; Baker Book House Company, 1981., Arbor, Michigan

This engraving shows how the Babylonian King is the physical manifestation of the sun-god Zeus. He is represented as one of the two pillars upon which the entire universe rests; the sun over the day and the northern star over the night. They work together ruling the entire universe. Upon his pillar is the pyramid with the point facing up, this represents the male body being the temple of the sun. It is the body of the man that is the physical temple which the sun-god Zeus manifests himself in through the ruler of the world. This is illustrated by the eight pointed sun touching the top of the pyramid. It shows that the sun-god has come down and has joined himself to the temple.

The second pillar represents his bride, the moon-goddess or the northern star. She is symbolized by the feminine pyramid pointing down in darkness with the crescent moon just above it. Together they are the completion of the two gods which rule over the day and the night. The entire host of heaven is under their command. The female is the embodiment of all of the stars, i.e. the host of heaven, which are controlled through her body. Her body is filled with the darkness of night, like the blanket of space upon which all the stars inhabit. They enter into her through her opening herself spiritually to them. Physically, she is a holy prostitute by willingly giving herself over to whosoever her father or the goddess instructs her to do. Spiritually she is a holy prostitute by giving herself over to the indwelling and use of all the angelic host. She is willingly used by them to do the bidding of her husband the sun-god, who is the ruler over her. Nebuchadnezzar believed that he was the sun-god and ruler over all of the earth. He believed that he controlled all of the earth and that through his wife, the holy prostitute, all of the host of heaven, (i.e. angelic forces) were at his disposal. This was not some new form of worship but is actually the basis from which all religions sprang.[113]

We first read of the sun and moon gods through human vessels in ancient Babylon where an astrology tower was built for specifically for the purpose of worshipping the sun, and moon, and all the host of heaven. The Egyptian Pharaoh believed himself to be the physical manifestation of the sun—god Ra and his priests were the manifestation of the moon-god, Iah, Thoth, Khonsu and Osiris. In the original form of Egyptian worship the moon-god had four names, each depicting one of its different phases of position in the sky. They also showed the four face of a cherub and

---

[113] Christianity is not a form of religion, Christianity is a relationship with the Lord Jesus Christ. Man walked with God and fellowshipped with God in the garden of Eden before the fall into sin. Religion is that which comes between man and the true God. The Holy Spirit of God restores us to fellowship with God.

how it could inhabit a man. It was not until later on in Egyptian history that Isis becomes known as the moon-goddess, prior to that, she was known as the star Sirius, the brightest star in the galaxy. As Sirius she was the brightest light in the night, thus ruling over all of the other stars in the heaven. Sirius is called the *Dog Star* and is the brightest in the constellation known as *Canis Major*, the Greater Dog. This idea of two bright lights to rule over the day and the night was from God's own hand. In the book of Genesis we read:

> "And God made two great lights; the greater light to rule the day, and the lesser light to rule the night: he made the stars also. And God set them in the firmament of the heaven to give light upon the earth, And to rule over the day and over the night, and to divide the light from the darkness: and God saw that it was good."[114]

This speaks of the two entities that would rule over all the others. It is later on in the worship of Nimrod that they began representing the masculine and the feminine, i.e. Nimrod and Semiramis. Many believed that Nimrod got

---

[114] Genesis 1:16-18

this idea from the original authority given to man in the Garden of Eden.

In the beginning God had given Adam federal headship over all creation. Adam personally named every animal and insect. It was his job to take care of every plant and animal. The angels were the servants God had given him so he could control and regulate the entirety of creation. Man lost this control when he willfully rebelled against God. Adam chose to obey the leading of a fallen angel and in doing this he lost his position and authority. This one act of rebellion forever opened Adam, Eve and all of their descendants to the power and disease of sin. Adam not only became infected with the disease of sin but he also lost his authority over the angelic forces and his position in Eden. Without the Shekinah glory of God upon Adam he was no longer able to control and regulate the heavens and earth, thus leaving it open to the power and influence of the devil and his entities.[115] This worship of the sun-god and northern star-goddess continued and spread to the entire world when the tower of Babel was destroyed and man's language was confounded. As man spread he took the worship of the sun and moon with him. The Phoenicians

---

[115] Genesis 3; Matthew 4:8-10: Heavens are plural as it describes the sky above the earth and also the stars and galaxies.

worshipped Baal and Baalite, the Greeks, Syrian, Romans, Persians all worshipped the sun and moon-god/'s. Even the name Allah finds its roots as the moon-god that married the sun goddess and all the stars were his daughters.[116]Many worldwide organizations are completely devoted to this form of worship. For instance, the Masonic Temple and brotherhood worship the god of light as their chief god with the eastern star as his wife and counterpart. In the worship of the Masonic Lodge and the Eastern Star they commune with the entire host of heaven to do their bidding. In the Masonic Bible the temple is pictured with the tower of Babel in the center as the main point to reach heaven through. It is the center of true worship to the practitioner that is why their order is called *the craft*. They seek to join the worship of the great light/Lucifer with the entire host of heaven through the tower of Babel and the lesser light the eastern star. Notice the two pillars of the sun and the eastern star that a person must go through to enter into the temple. This diagram shows that one must go through the sun and eastern star in order to be able to enter into the celestial heaven where they are then opened up to the worship of all the host of heaven, illustrated by the various

---

[116] http://www.biblebelievers.au/moongod.htm

levels of the astrology tower. This is the true Masonic Temple.

The Masonic form of worship is nothing other than pure Nimrod-Babylonian worship, which the Bible condemns.[117] The city Nimrod built for himself so the whole world could come and worship him is the same where the tower of Babel was located and it was named Babel. Babel does not mean confounding, as in languages. What it means is a confusing by mixing together, i.e. confusing by missing together all the false religions of the world. It was a place where they mixed together the concept of the true God, Who had created everything, with the sun-god, the northern star-god and the entire host of heaven, which were the creation of God.[118] It was the beginning of cooperate man, collectively giving themselves over to every spirit and every kind of sin. Once again man was searching for a way to become like God. In order to prevent the angelic corruption of the entire human race again; he would give each of the families a different language thus forcing them to scatter over the face of the earth.[119] As they spread with their new languages they took with them the knowledge and worship of the false gods.

---

[117] Acts 7:43; Revelations 14:8, 16:19, 17:5, 18:2,10, 21
[118] Romans 1:19-32
[119] Genesis 3:5

The only difference would be that now the name of Satan would be different in every language. Some would call him Baal, others Lucifer and still others Zeus or by some other name. This is why Ashtoreth is called the goddess of a thousand names.

Many people and pastors of churches read chapters six through ten of Genesis and never have a clue about what was really taking place in the valley of Shinar. The salvation of the mankind was at stake! Let me explain. Up until this point in history, there had only been one language.[120] God had given the command to Noah and his sons to go out and multiply, i.e., to have children so that they could fill the earth with men and woman who would be able to enjoy Him giving Him worship and glorify His name. God had directed them to geographically spread out so the entire earth would be filled with God's glory. In spreading out they would be able to do the work of replenishing the earth.[121] The witness of God was to cover the entire world. There was plenty of work involved in replenishing the earth. Everything would have to be replanted from the seeds they brought onto the ark. The work would have involved planting trees, raising crops for

---

[120] Genesis 11:1,6
[121] Genesis 9:1-3, 7-10 ; Numbers 14:21; Psalm 19:1-6, 22:27, 24:1, 33:8, 89:11

food sources for themselves and also the grazing animal groups. It also involved breeding and cultivating of livestock for personal consumption and also to be used in worship of God. Life would have been simple and full for the children of Noah but rather than obeying God, as they began to multiply, they started gathering together in the valley of Shinar for the purpose of building an astrology tower. The truth of the matter is this; sinful man does not like to retain God in their knowledge, because the Holy Spirit convicts us of our sins. Darkness will not come to the light lest their deed should ne reproved. Sinful man prefers to worship the creation rather than the Creator.[122] This was mans attempt to gain control over nature again.

As we learned earlier, man had lost the ability to rule over creation when Adam and Eve sinned. All of the children had learned from Noah, Shem, Ham and Japheth how it had been prior to the fall of man and now it was their desire to once again be able to communicate with angels, animals and nature. They were trying to reverse God's judgment which had severed this ability. One of the first greatest atrocities that would come from this unholy union of man and angel was the giving of their unborn

---

[122]Romans 1:21-25, 28; John 3:19-21

children over to angels as permanent hosts.[123] It was a joining together, at the genetic level of man and ancient entity creating a child that would be a giant among men, a nephilim.[124]

> *"There were giants in the earth in those days; and also after that, when the sons of God came in unto the daughters of men, and they bare children to them, the same became mighty men which were of old, men of renown."*[106]

The word used for giants in the above verse is the word Nephilim. It is the first time it is used in the Scriptures. This is the way that it worked.

The fallen angels had authority to enter into those who rejected the true God. By rejecting the true God they were embracing the gods of this world. When it says that the sons of God found the daughters of men favorable, what it meant was that the woman agreed to marry themselves to these fallen entities. They willingly gave themselves over to these fallen spirits and through their union were born the mighty men of old, the *hibbor*

---

[123] Matthew 24:38
[124] Genesis 6:4

gibborum en nephilim.[125]The parents would give their bodies over to angels, in a voluntary possession. They did this by giving vows of marriage to the unholy spirits, uniting them to their spirits. So when the man and woman came together in coition and at the moment of conception an angelic entity would enter into the fertilized egg, permanently attaching itself to the embryo, creating a Nephilim; a hybrid human-angel that would be a giant among men. As the child grew and developed it would have little awareness of the parasitic being within it. I propose to you; that just as in the days of Noah, the world was filled with Nephilim and those given over to the indwelling of fallen spirits, and it is the same today. People it's time to get your hearts ready because the Lord Jesus Christ is getting ready to return for His children before He once again destroys the world. The only difference will be that instead of destroying the world with water, this time it will be with fire.[126]

Friends, Nephilim are all around us today. In every mythological account, children of the gods with special abilities walked amongst men; these were nephilim. A child that is a nephilim will be nurtured internally by the spirit as

---

[125] This means an ancient entity genetically linked with flesh creating an human-angelic hybrid.
[126] Galatians 4:3; 2 Peter 3:10, 12

111

it grows. The spirit within the child will endow it with exceptional abilities while guiding it into habits and passions that will foster the traits and gifts of the angelic entity. The entity will also impose limiting factors upon the child's brain, separating the conscious so that each individual part of the conscious will be able to focus upon its specific talent. To those, that reject the literacy of God's word, this would be something good, something to be sought after. Christians want their children to have the indwelling of the Holy Spirit of the true God leading them into a closer walk with God evidenced in a life of faith and practice. But sadly, the person with a genetic attachment has very little chance of coming to know the Lord Jesus Christ and receiving the salvation he offers. This is because the indwelling entity creates a very strong demonic covering of darkness that can only be broken by prayer and fasting. See the following example of a young girl that had an evil spirit.

"And when they were come to the multitude, there came to him a certain man, kneeling down to him, and saying, Lord, have mercy on my son: for he is lunatic, and sore vexed: for oft times he falleth into the fire, and oft into the water. And I brought him to thy disciples, and they could not cure him. Then Jesus answered and said, O faithless and perverse generation, how long shall I be with you? how long shall I suffer you? bring him hither to me. And Jesus rebuked the devil; and he departed out of him: and the child was cured from that very hour. Then came the disciples to Jesus apart, and said, Why could not we cast him out? And Jesus said unto them, Because of your unbelief: for verily I say unto you, If ye have faith as a grain of mustard seed, ye shall say unto this mountain, Remove hence to yonder place; and it shall remove; and nothing shall be impossible unto you. Howbeit this kind goeth not out but by prayer and fasting."[127]

This type of union can only be broken by the power of Jesus Christ. The demonic stronghold that results from the genetic union provides the doorway for other members of the host of heaven to enter through. The goal of the entity is to separate the mind of the subject thereby gaining control over the person. This is done by enslaving their mind,

---

[127] Matthew 17:14-21; Other examples include: Matthew 5:21-28

body, soul and spirit. This happens through the act of dissociation.[128]

Dissociation is a splitting of the mind. That psyche splits can be into just two separate alternate personalities or in the case of poly-fragmentation; it can be thousands of splits. Through the act of dissociation the mind becomes fragmented. Each time the mind is split an angelic entity host will attach to the part that is fragmented and will then place a dark covering over it in order to keep it separated from the greater conscious. Like demonic wedges driven into the psyche these entities will use the sins against the person to continually split and separate the mind of the individual until it is fragmented like the stars in the heavens. Each of the angels will take a piece of the psyche , veiling it in their darkness until it becomes a separate point like one of the stars in the sky. Each of these little points of light, i.e. the fragments, will be separated by a dark covering. They do this to control the person, enslaving them, and seeking to forever damn the person so they are ultimately cast into hell for all eternity.[129] This is why the Nephilim had to be destroyed; there goal was to damn all of

---

[128] For a study on dissociation I recommend: "The Big Book on Dissociate Identity Disorder," by myself, Dr. Tom Knotts, Jr.

[129] Deuteronomy 32:22; 2 Samuel 22:6; Job 26:6; Psalm 9:17, 18:5, 55:15, 116:3; Proverbs 15:11, 24; Isaiah 28:18; Habakkuk 2:5; Matthew 10:28, **16:18**; Luke 16:23; Revelations 1:18, 6:8, 20:13-14

mankind with their unholy union![130] It is not the will of God to damn anyone; His desire is to see all mankind come to salvation. But God will not force anyone to accept his salvation but he does offer it to all, freely, as a gift of his grace.

"For God so love the world that he gave his only begotten Son, that whosoever believeth in him should not perish, but have everlasting life. For God sent not his Son into the world to condemn the world; but that the world through him might be saved. He that believeth on him is not condemned: but he that believeth not is condemned already, because he hath not believed in the name of the only begotten Son of God. And this is the condemnation, that light is come into the world, and men loved darkness rather than light, because their deeds were evil."[131]

Because of the sin of Adam every person born has born been cursed with death and the spirit of sin. But praise is to God the Father for sending Jesus Christ His Son, the second Adam to give us life, removing the curse of sin and

---

[130] Genesis 6:6-7
[131] John 3:16-19

death and giving us eternal life and peace.[132] Ever since Adam committed the first sin all mankind has been under condemnation but Jesus came to offer his own body as a sacrifice so that we could live. He took our place and paid the price for our sins in order to purchase us to himself. If you accept that sacrifice you can be saved from condemnation and death. Many say that those who are Nephilim are children of the Devil, and this is true. But I propose to you this truth; everyone is a child of the Devil until they day they ask God for forgiveness of their sins and then accept the salvation that God the Father offers us through the blood of Jesus Christ, His Son, our Savior.[133] A person only has to seek God with their whole heart to find Him.[134] This is what makes the hybrid of the Nephilim so heinous. The entity seeks to break and divide the heart, mind, will, and emotions of the individual, separating the mind and conscious between the various other spirits and then covering those pieces it in a dark veil. Its goal is to forever damn the individual. It would be important to remember the Devil is the Adversary of all mankind. The unholy union of fallen angels and humans is what led the

---

[132] Romans 5:6-21
[133] John 8:44; Romans 3:23, 25, 6:23, 10: 10,13; 1 John 2:2, 4:10; Hebrews 10
[134] Jeremiah 29:13; Psalm 119:2; Jeremiah 24:7

Lord God to destroy all of mankind, with the exception of Noah and his family with a worldwide flood! But you see Noah found grace in the eyes of the Lord. God had mercy on Noah and his family. Even though Noah's son Ham and his grandson brought the Nephilim across the flood with them God still loved and delivered them and he loves you and will do the same for you. My friend if you believe that you are a sinner and you also believe that Jesus died for your sins you can be saved. With your heart you believe and the result is your eternal salvation. If you need salvation would you please accept Jesus Christ as your Savior?

Pray this prayer:

Dear Heavenly Father, I know that I'm a sinner but I believe that Jesus died for my sins. I am asking you to forgive me of my sins and for Jesus to enter into my heart and to be the Lord of my life. I accept Jesus as my Savior and thank you for your salvation. In Christ Jesus Name I do pray, Amen.

If you prayed that prayer would you tell someone? Let them know you have given your life to Jesus Christ. This takes us to the next topic; the mind of the beast.

When the Beast takes over

Complete possession-transformation does not just happen. There is always a prior warning. There is a cause and there is an effect.

> *"All this came upon the king Nebuchadnezzar. ... he was driven from men, and did eat grass as oxen, and his body was wet with the dew of heaven, till his hairs were grown like eagles' feathers, and his nails like birds' claws."*[135]

We are finally to the part of the book where I will describe the actual demonic oppression of an individual. The following account is of a king becoming an ox; not just any king though. This was the king of Babylon; the ruler over all, the known world.

There is always a cause . . .

Boanthropy did not just come upon Nebuchadnezzar it was the judging act of God for not giving him the glory due his

---

[135] Daniel 4:28, 33

name. Just like Pharaoh of Egypt, Nebuchadnezzar considered himself to be the physical manifestation of the sun-god. He believed that he held the highest position in the order of godhood and that all his accomplishments were a result of his own divine power. He had conquered all the other gods of the world to include the God of the Israelites.[136] There was a problem with this; the Israelites were God's chosen people. The only reason Nebuchadnezzar had conquered anyone was that God had preplanned to use him to conquer the world and to bring his children into captivity for 70 years to punish their disobedience. It was God that had sent his people into Egypt, during the days of Jacob in order to make of them a nation prior to giving them the land that he had promised unto their fathers; a land that would be theirs forever.[137] It was the will of God that His children go into Egypt and it was also the will that his children go into Babylon as slaves. What was not his will, was for them to lose their identity of being His children nor to turn away from worshipping him. The captivity was to bring them back into a right relationship with God. It was not His will for them to embrace the worship of the heathen gods nor to give

---

[136] Daniel 1:1-3
[137] Genesis 12:2, 46:3-4; Deuteronomy 4:5-8; Exodus 32:13; Jeremiah 7:7

reverence to the false sun-god manifested by these world rulers.[138] Israel's disobedience was by not observing the law of letting the land rest every seventh year. God was keeping track of the years that they owed the land rest. The land was to have its Sabbath. Since they owed seventy years of rest to the land God had them conquered, made captives and then taken back to Babylon so the land could have its rest.[139]

Here is where the problem happened; both of these world rulers made the mistake of trying to force the people of God to worship them. Caesar, though he thought he was also the sun-god, forced the entire world to worship him; that is everyone except the Jews. Caesar knew the Jews would die before they would worship him. He also knew that the history showed that bad things happened to world rulers that forced the worship of these Jewish people. Pharaoh learned the hard way. Because of his refusal to acknowledge the true God and to release his children to go and worship him all of Egypt was destroyed. To protect his children from complete idolatry Egypt and its gods were destroyed and the king of Babylon was struck down, proving to the world that the true God rules over everything

---

[138] Psalm 111:9; Leviticus 19:30, 26:2,
[139] Leviticus 26:34; Jeremiah 25:1-12, 29:10; Daniel 9:2; Zechariah 7:5

and He does whatsoever He chooses.[140] By forcing God's children, the Jewish nation into following his idolatrous form of worship, he was struck down![141] The true God will never share his glory with anyone else.[142] Because of this great sin he had to be judged. There was a cause!

---

[140] Exodus 5:2, 10:7; Daniel 3:5, 10, 15, 4:32, 34-37

[141] Exodus 5:2, Pharaoh believed he was the supreme manifestation of the god of this world and that all of the other gods were under him. He believed that if the God of Moses was real, he would have personally known him, and would have been over him. Daniel 4:28-30

[142] Exodus 29:43; Numbers 14:20-23; Psalm 3:3, 62:7; Isaiah 42:8, 48:11, 66:18-19

There is an effect . . .

"The same hour was the thing fulfilled upon Nebuchadnezzar: and he was driven from men, and did eat grass as oxen, and his body was wet with the dew of heaven, till his hairs were grown like eagles' feathers, and his nails like birds' claws."[143]

In the previous chapter we showed how there was a reason for the hand of God to move against Nebuchadnezzar. He was even warned of what would happen if he did not repent. Well from the above reading it is quite obvious that Nebuchadnezzar did not take the warning of God seriously; he was judged.

Imagine for just a moment how it must have been. Here is the mighty king of Babylon walking through his palace and praising himself for all of his great accomplishments but while in mid-sentence, he suddenly goes silent and drops to his hands and knees and lets out a low and long mooooo sound and begins acting like an ox! I can't begin to think of how those around him would have responded. All reason had left him. His mind was completely gone. He was not some raving mad man, no;

---

[143] Daniel 4:33

instead his mind, body, soul and spirit had become that of an ox. An ox is a form of cattle so if you can't picture an ox think of a large docile bull. Try and imagine how his counselors and servants must have felt? Think of the fear that would have came over them, as the man who was supposed to be the sun-god over all of the earth, the man that they worshipped as, the god over all gods, was crawling around on the ground looking for his next mouthful of grass.[144]

It had not been that long ago that this same king had erected a 70 foot statue of himself in the plain of Dura.[145] It was to be one of the wonders of the world, like the hanging gardens of Semiranius that he had built for his wife Amity; except this statue spoke of his greatness. It was a testament of the greatest Babylonian king to ever rule the world, something that would for centuries to come. Its splendor must have been magnificent. The cost of the gold alone by today's standards would have been in the billions! But what was money? He, as the ruler of the whole world owned everybody and everything? He did not just ask for people to acknowledge him for his accomplishments, no; he demanded their worship. Those that would not fall down

---

[144] Daniel 3
[145] Dura was a province of Babylon

and worship him would be put to death![146] It had not been that long ago that he had commanded all mankind to fall down and worship the image he had built of himself. I will make this statement once again because it bear repeating; God will not share His glory with anyone! The faithfulness of God's children is very dear unto the Lord, for He is a jealous God.[147] God chose to show the world that He was the true God, not Nebuchadnezzar. To do this He personally came down and entered the fiery furnace preserving the life of his three faithful servants, Shadrack, Meshak and Abednigo. These three faithful Israelites told the king that they would rather be put to death than to fall down before his statue.[148] For their faithfulness Christ personally came down and walked through the fires with them. Everyone that was close enough to see inside the fiery furnace saw the true God walking with his children. Nebuchadnezzar even acknowledge Him as the God that could deliver his children unlike any other God. He even commanded all the world to acknowledge the God of these three Hebrew servants but Nebuchadnezzar still did not worship him as the true God.

---

[146] The anti-Christ will do the same thing in the end of time; Revelations 13, 14:9,11

[147] Exodus 20:5, 34:14,; Deuteronomy 4:24, 5:9. 6:15; Joshua 24:19

[148] Daniel 3:14-28

In spite of seeing the true God's delivering power Nebuchadnezzar still did not acknowledge Him as being the God over all the earth. He acknowledged that these three men did serve a great God, a God that could deliver his servants like no other but that was their God not his. For this great sin he was struck down by God losing all semblance of humanity. This insanity lasted for seven years.

Upon first glance it would appear that the only thing that was affected was his mind. But this was not the case, the transformation went much deeper. Notice the description, it began with his heart:

"Let his heart be changed from man's, and let a beast's heart be given unto him; and let seven times pass over him."

The heart is the part of man known as the soul. It is the heart that works in conjunction with the mind to make all of our decisions. When the Bible says let his heart be changed from a man's and let a beast's heart be given unto him what it is literally saying is this:[149]

---

[149] This is one of the 17 verses in the Bible that was written in Aramaic instead of Hebrew. This is because it was Nebuchadnezzar's personal testimony written by his own hand.

Let his heart and mind be put to sleep, since he is a man, and place within him the mind and heart of a living thing.

The "*living thing*," spoken of in this verse is a cherub, an angel with four faces.[150] It was an angel that was given the authority to take over Nebuchadnezzar's mind, heart and body. This punishment of God was administered by the decree/command of the watchers. The watchers were the guardian angels God had assigned to watch over his children in Babylon.[151] The text implies that god's children had been pouring out their hearts unto in prayer to deliver them from the un-godly sins and practices of the kingdom of Babylon. They desired the ability to worship and serve him as he ordained but this was being hindered by the cruelty of their captors. This punishment was carried out in answer to their prayers. It happened at the time that God had already pre-appointed. God knows the end before the beginning.[152] The holy ones mentioned in this verse are his

---

[150] Living things are spoken of in several places in the Scriptures: Ezekiel 1:5, 13-15, 19,3:13; Revelations 4:6, 8-9 , 5:6, 8, 11, 4 , 6:1,6, 8, 7:11, 14:3, 15:7, 18:13, 19:4. Beasts is the word used for angel that looks like a created animal.

[151] Psalm 34:7

[152] Isaiah 46:10; Daniel 8:19, 11:35; Revelations 21:6, 22:13

saints, i.e. his children that were praying unto Him.[153] God in His mercy wanted Nebuchadnezzar to repent. God is not willing that any person perishes but is longsuffering waiting for them to repent.[154] He had warned him in a dream 12 months prior to being struck down that this would happen to him if he did not turn from his wicked ways but Nebuchadnezzar did not believe the word of the Lord and for this he suffered judgment.[155] Remember the warning Daniel had given him in the interpretation of the dream.

"Wherefore, O king, let my counsel be acceptable unto thee, and break off thy sins by righteousness, and thine iniquities by shewing mercy to the poor; if it may be a lengthening of thy tranquillity."[156]

Despite seeing the power of God in the lives of Daniel, Hananiah, Mishael, and Azariah, Nebuchadnezzar did not repent. He acted like a brute beast and in a ironic twist of

---

[153] Ephesians 6:18; Philippians 4:6; God's children are called holy, i.e. saints. In Revelations 6:9-11 we read of his saints in heaven petitioning him to move against the anti-Christ and the world system to deliver his children. God tells them to be patient for he has an appointed time in which his judgment will be released upon the world.
[154] 2 Peter 3:9
[155] Daniel 4:29
[156] Daniel 4:27

fate he was turned into one![157] His heart and mind were put into a state of sleep without any aspect of conscious and a angelic cherub entered into his body and took over everything. In psychology this is called a state of fugue. Fugue is when time stops for a persons' conscious allowing another personality take to over. While in a state of fugue the person is unaware of anything that is happening. Notice the description; he was transformed into the likeness of a cherub.

> *"The same hour was the thing fulfilled upon Nebuchadnezzar: and he was driven from men, and did eat grass as oxen, and his body was wet with the dew of heaven, till his hairs were grown like eagles' feathers, and his nails like birds' claws"[158]*

He had the face of a man, the claws of an eagle, the mane of a lion and the internal organs of an ox. He had become completly possessed[159] and transformed by a four faced cherub. If you remember the case studies mentioned

---

[157] Jude 10
[158] Daniel 4:33
[159] Ownership was given to the angel to take control of every part of his being.

previously, the patients suffering from boanthropy lived entirely off of grass and water. They had no other food source and yet they were perfectly healthy and happy. Actually the physicians state that the man's strength and constitution had increased considerably while suffering from the boanthropy. Both of the victims also had increased hair and nail growth. This sounds exactly like the description of Nebuchadnezzar. He had become an animal. There was no kingdom for him, no people to rule, neither worries nor cares, he was just another mindless beast wandering the fields of Babylon.

He was driven from men

Nebuchadnezzar had become life a wild animal and just like a wild animal he had no ability to live in society. If you have ever seen cattle, they go to the bathroom anywhere-anytime they want to. You cannot have cattle in your home they need to be in the fields where there unclean lifestyles will fertilize the fields not destroy the palace. He would be going to the bathroom when ever and where ever he chose with no inhibitions. Like a wild ox he would have been scratching himself against whatever looked good to him. Farmers in the region where I live have a fence around all of their trees in their fields because if they don't protect the trees the cattle will rub up against them, removing all of the bark and killing the tree. Could you imagine Nebuchadnezzar in a palace filled with priceless objects? If he got the urge to exfoliate, i.e. scratch the itch through rubbing against something the amount of damage he would cost would be incredible. This is why you do not let a bull go into a china shop nor do you allow a ox like beast to live with people in the palace. On the brighter side because of his condition he would have much more preferred the solitude of grazing in the fields around Babylon. That is where he would have felt at home. In the two cases mentioned before both of the patients were left to graze, eat and sleep on the grounds around the hospitals. That was where they felt most natural. It was where they belonged and it made them happy.

He ate grass as an ox

The transformation went much deeper than just his skin, nails and hair; it changed his digestive track completely. Friends, a cow or an ox can live entirely off of grass, the human digestive track cannot. There are certain vitamins and minerals that we simply cannot glean from chewing a cud. The reason why Nebuchadnezzar and the two mental patients could live entirely off grass is because their gastro-intestinal systems had been changed by the indwelling spirit. They had changed the structure of his organs. Considering this; angels changed the physical structure of non-living things into living things in Pharaohs court; so changing the organs of a living mans into a living beasts would have been no problem for them.

When a person undergoes a complete transformation into an animal, it is not just the exterior cosmetics that are changed. Their organs are also changed. I have personally known a man that could not survive on anything but human blood. He was a literal vampire. Until he came to deliverance from the spirit that had possessed him, he lived entirely off of human blood. Others that believed he was an incarnate vampire willingly gave him their blood to drink. He told me that he had an endless supply of people waiting in line wanting to give him their blood to drink. They worshipped him as a god. He became a vampire by going through a high level cultic ritual where he invited a demonic spirit into himself, giving it complete control over him. In exchange he got certain abilities from the spirit. With his demonic possession were many side effects. For instance, he could not stand to be around garlic. It would make him violently ill. If he came into the house and there was garlic in the home he would immediately know it, and would have a violent reaction.[160] When he tried to eat anything but blood he would get sick and vomit it back up. For nearly three years the only food source he had was human blood. It was not just a source of food, for him, it was his life. He craved the blood. He told me that what had driven him to seek help was the uncontrollable thirst for human blood that would come over him. He said the lust for blood had became so great that when he would drive down the road if he saw someone out walking alone it was all he could do, to not pull over and assault them for their blood.

---

[160] I worked with a woman that was possessed by a spirit of vampirism and she somehow knew that I had garlic in my home and she would not enter until I had removed it from my house.

Another negative side effect was that he could not go out into the daylight. Sunlight would cause him to have an immediate blistering reaction to his skin. He worked at night and would only go out at night. It was only after coming to salvation and renouncing being a vampire that he was set free from this curse. Nebuchadnezzar's mind and body were also changed so that for a period of seven years the only thing he wanted to eat was grass and to drink water and it completely sustained him.

He took on the image of the beast

The transformation Nebuchadnezzar experienced changed him into something other than human; a combination of man, animal and angel, in his case a cherub. The Bible describes a particular type of cherub as having four faces:[161]

"Also out of the midst thereof came the likeness of four living creatures. And this was their appearance; they had the likeness of a man. And every one had four faces, and every one had four wings. And their feet were straight feet; and the sole of their feet was like the sole of a calf's foot: and they sparkled like the colour of burnished brass. And they had the hands of a man under their wings on their four sides; and they four had their faces and their wings. Their wings were joined one to another; they turned not when they went; they went every one straight forward. As for the likeness of their faces, they four had the face of a man, and the face of a lion, on the right side: and they four had the face of an ox on the left side; they four also had the face of an eagle."[162]

---

[161] The Bible also lists cherub as having 1 face, 2 faces, 3 faces and 4 faces. Daniel 8:16, 10:5; Luke 1:19, 26; Ezekiel 10:14, 28:16, 41:18;
[162] Ezekiel 1:5-10

These angels had the likeness of a man, in other words they were in the shape of a man. That is why they had straight feet like a man but the soles of their feet were like the hooves of a calf. They also had hands under their wings like that of a man. They each had four faces; the face of a man, the face of a lion, the face of an ox and the face of an eagle. These were the four faces of a cherub.

Nebuchadnezzar ate grass like an ox; his digestive track had been changed into that of an ox. His body was wet with the dew of heaven, as the great lion he slept without fear upon the open ground with his hair long and thick like a lion's mane down his neck and back. His hair grew thick and long upon his body until it spread out like the feathers of an eagle. His finger nails grew thick and long and curled under his hands like the talons of an eagle. His face, though the face of a man had lost all aspects of humanity. He had all the attributes of a cherub.

At the end of seven years, Nebuchadnezzar was given back his mind, body and heart. When the angel left him, his mind and body were restored back into their original form with one exception; he had complete knowledge and memories of everything that had transpired over the last seven years. I have personally witnessed an individual that was completely possessed by the spirit of an animal. Though his eyes were closed he could see everything. He was in every way a snarling tiger. He exhibited supernatural strength and reflexes that were, not only cat like, but were unbelievably fast. After being freed from the spirits he told me that he could hear the voices of those trying to set him free, commanding the demonic spirits in him but it was as if he was trapped inside a building, only being able to hear through the walls. He could not see anything in the room where his body was. He could not cry out, his vocal chords and mouth were being controlled by the spirits. He was helpless to help himself. During the entire ordeal, (over three hours long) he said that he had been trapped inside of the Shaolin Temple in the Henan Province of China; which was inside of him. He had given himself over to be a shaolin priest and practiced voluntary possession by the animal spirits of the forms that he practiced. Now in the moment of terror those spirits had completely possessed him and were keeping him locked in the temple he had given himself over to. He said that they had him positioned in the center of the temple and all the animal spirits were encircling him, not allowing him to move, speak or respond in any way. They had possessed his body, mind and heart. All he could do, was in his mind plead for help!

Deliverance came to that young man by the hands of a skilled counselor who could tell that he was possessed. The man said the counselor had confronted him as to why he was leaving a seminar early. It was interesting as soon as the speaker began praying this man got up and began pacing the back of the room. He said that he could not stand it, he kept hearing in his mind to get out of there! So after a few minutes he went to leave and this counselor stepped in front of him and asked him why he was leaving. He said that it was at that moment that he lost all ability to speak but he heard his mouth open and say, "Hi my name is ------------, I'm sorry but I have an emergency -------- and need to leave. The man said, "no you don't I command you to be bound, who am I talking with?" He said that it was at that moment that he was completely possessed. He woke up nearly an hour later with this counselor and several others working with him binding the spirits and praying on his behalf for them to release him. He said that he could hear them but he could not respond because they had him trapped in the shaolin temple in his mind and were circling him. Three hours later he was finally set free of all the spirits. The counselors said they had never seen a person shape shift before but this young man had actually begun changing into a tiger in front of them. At one point he picked up a piece of furniture weighing around 250 pounds by one end, (it was 8 feet long and not built to be lifted by one end) and he had it in the air about to hit them before they bound him again. This man had been raised in a cultic family that practiced Masonic science and alchemy and eastern star religion. He had been given over to martial arts training at the age of nine and was personally trained to be a shaolin priest for over nine years. The combination of all this cultism came with a price; they ended up completely possessing the man and if it had not been for the insight and leading of the Holy Spirit of those counselors he would not have been set free. He would probably be in a mental institution today. This brings us to the next subject, shap shifters.

Shape Shifters

Shape shifter is a term that is used to identify a person that has the ability to change; both their mental frame of mind and their belief about themselves. It does not always imply the physical body being changed. The majority of shape shifters change only in spirit and mind but there are a few that do change physically. Whatever a person believes will set the foundation for how they live their life. When a person believes themselves to be something other than human or a combination producing a hybrid it will affect them in some way. In the realm of the shape shifter, the belief of being something more than human, affects their body's ability to function and perform in uncommon ways. It can be something as simple as increased intuitiveness or reflexive reactions so quick that they appear to be precognitive. This is called enhancement of the senses. Not every shape shifter experiences enhancement of the senses some actually become baser in their instincts, taking on the more rudimentary characteristics and traits of an animal. I have seen men go from states of normal human social interaction to becoming an animal in the matter of moments. It was like a switch had been flipped. In the martial arts I witnessed practitioners that lost all aspects of humanity, becoming the animal of the forms they had mastered.[163] They could go in and out of these animal states at the snap of a finger. Let me give you an example: While at a social gathering a person I knew walked up between me and three of my friends. This man was somewhat of a bully and was considered to be very good as a fighter. He made the mistake of attempting to throw a punch at one of the men standing there with us but before he even lifted his arm the other person had hit him so fast and hard that it happened before anyone had a chance to see or even know what had happened. I remember seeing the look in his eyes, though very much smaller, (about 150 pounds) he was as hard as a rock and his eyes had turned completely black; they were cold and lifeless. He had shape shifted into a powerful hybrid. Upon being helped up the man who had started it told me that he could not understand how the second man knew he was going to hit him. He was planning to sucker punch the small friend of mine standing there him but something triggered and switched in him before he had the chance. My small friend hit the man so hard it split both his lips and cheek open. He had to go get

---

[163] This was a common practice in the deeper level of the esoteric of the eastern martial arts.

stitches. The power and speed he showed were staggering. By the way the small man did not practice martial arts, boxing or any skill. He was a natural shape shifter. He said that whenever someone would try to hurt him, he would change; becoming, as he put it, a bull dog. He said it was completely uncontrollable. That his body would just snap and do things without his control He said that when these experiences came over him that everything would move in slow motion and that he would feel like steel with an unbelievable abundance of strength. In his mind he was a big pit bull dog that was undefeatable.

When a person shape shifts their external physical appearance will not always change, but their eyes always do. The eyes tell the story of what is happening inside of them. The martial artists that I would watch all had this one characteristic in common; their eyes became cold and dead and the mechanics of their mannerisms completely changed into the animal they had become. They moved as the animal moved. They were precise and calculated. It was not an act or performance by someone trained to act or perform but rather it was the spirit of the animal had entered into them, taking over their mind and body. This is the nature of the shape shifter. The shape shifter is a type of theriomorph, one that has the ability to summon a spirit into their body and then to give their body over to the will of the spirit.

Shape shifter come in a variety of types. Because they have an indwelling spirit they are sometime identified as being channel'ers rather than shape shifters. But that is a false classification as they do not channel the spirit through themselves. A medium is someone who allows a spirit to speak through them or that serves as a channel for a spirit. If the spirit indwells the person, taking control over their mind and body in a controlled form of possession, than they are a shape shifter. I define a shape shifter as this:

Shape is something that has form but cannot be clearly seen, i.e. the spirit of man, animal or entity. Shifter means to change or exchange something for something else.

So a shape shifter is someone that's body, mind, spirit or any combination of the three is changed or exchanged with something else.

Due to the purity of the definition this would include the realm of religion as there are many individuals all over the world that experience the exchange of spiritual control. In many ritualistic forms of worship it is the only way they

143

can worship their gods. In many charismatic circles of Christianity the participants mistake the filling of the Holy Spirit of the true God for the possessing of an un-holy spirit of the world, i.e. a fallen angelic entity. This makes them a shape shifter. Because of the limited use of the definition the term shape shifter has become synonymous with lycanthropy or some other type of morph but in reality its inclusiveness is quite widespread encompassing every religion and region of the world. Next I would like to explain the difference between a shape shifter and a morph.

The Morph

A Morph is a completely different type of theriomorph than the shape shifter. A morph is a human being that has obtained the ability to draw power from a totem animal, at times even acquiring its physical characteristics. A totem is an object that is empowered through the worship and devotion that is given to it. For instance in many pagan religions it is common for the image of their god to be carved into stone or wood in order to be the center of their focused worshipped. In the book of judges there are many instances where the Israelites fell into the worship of idols and images.[164] The morph believes that the spirit of a god enters enter into the object when worship and devotion is offered unto it. Below is a short list of totem types:

1) Eskimo and Indian Totem poles
2) Catholic relics and icons
3) Religious masks
4) Cursed Objects or relics of power, (this includes jewelry, clothing, furniture, anything of value)

---

[164] Genesis 31:19; Exodus 32:4-35; Leviticus 26:30; Numbers 33:52; Judges 18; 1 Kings 4:9—23; 2 Kings 10, 17, 23; Hosea 11:2, 13:2; Amos 5:26

5) Bones and constructed items of bone
6) Stone glyphs or images in stone like gargoyles or the green man image

The totem can be something as large as one of the monolithic heads on eastern Island or as small as a tooth from the mouth of a person that has died. I remember being consulted by the local law enforcement on a case they had of grave robbery. The Chief asked me if there was a reason why someone would dig up a grave and steal a part of the body. I had to answer yes. In this case it was the grave of a person that had been hung for murder over a hundred years prior to the day of the vandalism. The only thing taken from the grave was the hand. They did not remove the jewelry from the other hand which had the Chief puzzled. I told the Chief that the hand was most likely stolen to be used as a totem of power by the leader of a local cult. He acknowledged that they had found evidence that some unknown ritual or ceremony had happened in the area.

Totems come in all shapes and sizes. If the object is given reverence, devotion or worship it can be a source of great power for the morph. The totem itself is nothing more than a medium device between a spiritual entity and the person seeking power. In many types of religion they will use various forms of jewelry as items for empowering. These are lesser aspects of totem worship. By giving reverence, fear, devotion or worship to the item or the entity, that the item is associated with, it allows the channeling of the spirit through the item into the person. Acts 7:40-43 tells of the Israelites using a totem.

"Saying unto Aaron, Make us gods to go before us: for as for this Moses, which brought us out of the land of Egypt, we wot not what is become of him. And they made a calf in those days, and offered sacrifice unto the idol, and rejoiced in the works of their own hands. Then God turned, and gave them up to worship the host of heaven; as it is written in the book of the prophets, O ye house of Israel, have ye offered to me slain beasts and sacrifices by the space of forty years in the wilderness? Yea, ye took up the tabernacle of Moloch, and the star of your god Remphan, figures which ye made to worship them: and I will carry you away beyond Babylon."

The word Remphan speaks of a small idol they kept in their homes as an idol/totem of worship. For this God judged them in order to prove to them that he was the only true

God. It was His desire that they seek His Holy Spirit, not the gods of this world. Morphs are more than idol worshippers they become spiritually linked with the object of power that they serve. The totem is a cursed object. Like all idolatry is will seek to enslave the person, taking their heart through worship and devotion.

While on this subject of cursed objects, I would like to point out that there are many people who fall victim to evil entities by buying or inheriting cursed items. I have worked with individuals that have become spiritually oppressed after obtaining a cursed object. When an item it given to an entity in a ritual, the entity has the authority to use the item howsoever it desires. Evil entities will use the item for evil, and by the way they are all evil angels. No good angel of God's would ever try to take worship or devotion from Him.

Totems are not measured in strength by size or stature. Some very powerful relics have been discovered in the Hawaiian Islands that were only a few inches in height. A friend of mine from Bible College attested to the demonic spiritual influence of the tiny totems found in the islands. At the time I did not believe in their abilities to do anything but he was from the Islands and when the subject came up, he became sober and warned me of the seriousness of these items of worship. He said that an incredible amount of evil could be generated from these tiny idols. I saw what he was talking of first hand several decades later.

While pastoring my second church I had a young couple come to me for counseling. They had been referred to me and even though they lived almost 1500 miles away they drove for two days to come and see me. What had happened was that an incubus, which is a demon of sexual violence, and rage, had begun manifesting and assaulting the couple. By assaulting them, I don't mean in wisps of air or things moving around their home; this entity was fully manifesting and physically assaulting them, which included sexually assaulting the woman and when the man tried to stop it from hurting his wife it threw him through the air. At one point the demon manifested while the man was in the shower and bit a chunk of flesh out of his chest. These spiritual manifestations started happening shortly after the couple returned home from their honeymoon vacation in the Virgin Islands. Through prayer, God revealed the source of the demonic attack was two cursed bracelets they were wearing on the arms. While on their honeymoon they saw a voodoo priest's shop and thought it would be a neat place to check out. In America you can novelty shops filled with all kinds of weird stuff and to them it seemed like a harmless place to check out. The only problem was that this was a real voo-doo priest over that area. They went through the shop and bought themselves a pair of bracelets as souvenirs. It turned out that the bracelets were cursed objects that had been devoted to one of the pagan gods that the priest worshipped. By buying the bracelets in full knowledge of the pagan priest's profession, and then wearing them; it allowed a demon of hatred and violence to fully manifest and assault them. While they were in my office the demon manifest in front of me. The man screamed and ran from the room while his wife's chair was lifted up into the air and an invisible force began physically assaulting her. Though I could not see it, I commanded it to be bound but the abuse did not stop. Now realize something was holding her and I could see the imprints upon her face and body as something was striking her very hard! As she was screaming I cried out to the Lord to send holy angels to come and grab it and to hold it so it could not hit her anymore. Her chair went back down to the ground and the entity manifested right in front of me. It was only about 14 inches high. It looked like a dragon/humanoid that was red and black. I told it out loud, "you cannot hit me I have the shield of faith."[165] It replied, "you have no faith." I said, "your right, I'm scared." I lifted up my hands and prayed out loud telling God that I was afraid of this creature and then I asked God to forgive me and to place His holy armor upon me. I then asked the entity if I now had the shield of faith and it said, "Yes." I then asked it why it did not attack me and it said, "I didn't have permission!" I then called the man back into the room and lead them in prayer to God asking for forgiveness for going into the voodoo shop/temple and to cleanse them and the bracelets, removing all curses upon them and the bracelets, severing all unholy ties and attachments and then to send the entity where he would command it to go by the voice of his Holy Spirit. After praying the entity never appeared again. The two bracelets were cursed objects that were devoted to a demon of sexual violence and hatred. They were designed to be given to a person's enemy not to be worn by the buyer.

The most powerful aspect of the totem is that is opens a doorway for channeling an entity or spirit into the worshipper. If the totem is cursed it will seek to create a doorway into those within its sphere of influence in an attempt to either inhabit or to torment. This doorway can be

---

[165] The armor of God listed in Ephesians 6

created by fear, reverence, lust, or any other emotion. The purpose of totems is to create a symbiotic relationship with the host in order to give them enhanced or supernatural abilities. Mediums have forms of totems in the object they use. For instance the tea cup of a medium gives them the ability to glimpse tiny bits of a persons' life. A water bowl and a crystal ball are two types of totems used to enable a person to see places that are far away.

Another way that totems work is in exchanging spirits with animals. Shamans, medicine men and other totemists can use the totem in a reverse channeling method where they astral project their spirit out of their own bodies and into the body of the animal or other creature that is symbolized by the totem. When the person leaves their body and enters into an animal, the demonic entity that enabled them to leave their body will then join them with the spirit of the animal. The two spirits will unify into an anthropomorphic hybrid. The person can use all of the senses of the animal, hearing, sight, smell and even the passions that the animal feels while in their body. Those who project into animals often will vividly describe how exhilarating it is to run with the wolves or how it incredibly exciting it is to be flying with the hawk. Seeing the world though the eyes of an animal is an incredible experience but it can also have its dangers. First of all, it is a very addicting practice. Once a person begins going down the path of projecting into animals, every time they come back to their bodies they will bring back more of the aspects of the animal with them. The more a person projects the greater the possibility that they will become an animal in their mind. They will be forever lost in the mind of the animal. When that happens they lose all desire to be human and they become consumed by the spirit of the animal. Also while being in the body of the animal, great care must be taken, if the animal's body dies before the human spirit breaks free than they will both experience the pain of death. The trapped person will feel and experience the death of the animal as if it is their own. The result is that both the animal and the human will die.

Using a totem for projecting is a very dangerous path to tread. The more time that a person spends out of their body projected into an animal's body, the greater the chance that the feelings and emotions of the animal will overtake them and they will forget who they are. They will lose their sense of self. The demonic spirit that projects with the person into the animal will seek to consume the persons mind, slowly gaining ground until it crosses the point of no return where the animal takes over the human.

The person will lose their personal identity to that of the animal. When the person becomes consumed by the animal, they completely forget that they ever were a human being and the demon will take possession of their physical body. When a person's body suffers this type of possession than madness will take over their mind. When their body dies, the silver cord attaching their spirit to their body will snap and their soul will return to God, Who gave it.

The same type of warning must be heeded when the entity of the idol or totem enters into the individual. The danger lies in the possibility of complete possession. The demon will try to consume and entrap the mind of the person until it completely takes over their body and possesses the person. A word of warning: The more times that they allow the spirit to enter into their body, the greater the chance that the spirit will take complete possession of them. This happens in high level martial arts where the spirit of the animal slowly consumes the practitioner until they are completely consumed by the spirit of the animal. Projecting in and out of one's body is a very dangerous game that should not be played.

The Use of a Familiar

Throughout history witches and cultists have used their personal pets as familiars. A familiar is a spiritual entity that is assigned to influence a family member or a family line. In those family lines where they have an affinity with their familiar, it becomes a sort of assistance or gopher to the person. Those in the occult will use the familiar spirit for a number of things. It can be a spiritual guide, consultant, and spy or just about anything the person needs. High level cultist also use objects like necklaces, pendants and statues as medium points with their familiars. Familiars are the spiritual servants of the cultic family line. They are used in every type of craft from tea reading, palm reading, astrology, tarot card reading, water witching, etc. If it is a form of the occult there is a familiar associated with the practice. Familiars in plain language are spirits that are assigned to or attached to genial family lines. They can easily enable a person to project into any animal or plant the person desires. Though they can be the source of a person becoming a theriomorph they generally will not have the power to cause transformation in the individual.

The true theriomorph does not just transfer spirits but actually changes spiritually and physically. They are a physical representation of one of the gods of this world. It can be any representation of nature, plant, angel or man. In cases of generational spirits the person will be born with the spirit already inhabiting them. The entity will reside inside of the person until the opportunity for change presents itself. I have read of individuals that were able to become dolphins, crocodiles, and even sharks. I personally believe the yeti and other forms of the big foot are theriomorphs that change back into their human form. This is why they are never found.

In the realm of dark magic there are incredible feats that can be accomplished. There are stories of individuals that can take on the form of any animal, whether it be a cat, bird, lion, bear, or wolf. These theriomorphs are different than totemic morphs. These shifters do not need an idol or totem in order to achieve their desired result. They accomplish the feat through physical projection into, or through, a familiar spirit. Recall that a familiar is an animal that has a spirit that is attached to, or assigned to, a family line or a particular individual. The familiar can be a cat, rat, bear, dog, wolf, lion, tiger, hawk, falcon, owl or any animal. This also applies to those who can become, "shadow animals." Here is the true realm of the witch, shaman, or cultist.[166]

The shadow animal is a particular form of wraith used in necromancy. One example is the *"nightmare."* The nightmare is a spirit that appears like a dark horse, usually a black stallion. The nightmare lets the person travel on its back at an incredible rate of speed and over immense distances. It is a controlled form of astral projection but is limited to the plane of earth. The person has the ability to use shadow animals can also attach their spirit to dark entities such as wraiths or shades and then travel with them in the night. A wraith is an evil demonic entity that's supernatural ability is to physically manifest as a solid form in the dark. For instance the two bracelets that the couple had bought at the voo-doo shop had some of the essence of the priest attached to the incubus/wraith in the bracelets. A wraith is limited in the day light, only being able to exist for very short periods of time if light is present. While in this form, the evil of the entity will seek to consume the consciousness of the host, driving them to do unspeakable things to others. This is where the stories of the doppelganger arise from. It is an evil twinning with a dark spirit or wraith. This is the darkest of the arts those that

---

[166] Necromancers can also do this type of magic.

practice it will end with it ultimately being their demise. It will seek to totally consume the practitioner. I would like to warn all readers to stay away from any type of magic no matter how innocent it may seem. If you or a person you know are having demonic encounters and are in need of help I urge you to seek out a Christian Counselor that believes in the influence of fallen angels and also understands how to lead the person to freedom. If you are struggling with any of the aforementioned and I can be of help to you please do not hesitate to call upon me. I can be reached through my website:

www.SRA-DIDFreedomInChrist.com

Chapter Three: The Clan

I would like to take this final chapter to address the subject of the clan. When addressing the subject of the theriomorph the definition of a clan is this; a specific group, family or family line that manifests particular deity. For instance, there are many pagan groups that share the idea of spiritism. They raise and train their children in how to give themselves over to spirit inhabitation. It can be an isolated group that worships a particular animal type and thereby they give themselves over to the spirit of that particular animal. History records many tribes and groups that have dressed in garments and ornaments linking them spiritually to a specific animal type. For example:

- the clan of the cat
- the clan of the cave bear [these tend to live solitary lives]
- the clan of the rat
- the pack of the wolf
- the affinity of the turtle

In families that worship the sun-god and star-goddess they seek to manifest the god/goddess in their children. They will give their children over in ceremonies of devotion to the god, usually sealing the pact with a sacrifice of some type. Then after the spirit enters the child they will raise it up in a lifestyle of worship to the entity they serve. These families consider themselves to be the elite of the earth and like Caesar and Pharaoh they practice incest. They raise their daughters to be holy prostitutes for the complete manifestation of the goddess. This is the manifestation of the deity, the holy prostitute. They seek to link the child to the gods of nature by having them become some form of a beast. It can be a werewolf, pig, great cat or any type of creature. They are called a clan because they continue the linage of being a theriomorph. Some of these lines have been in existence since the days of Noah, dating back to Ham, Canaan or Nimrod. According to tradition there were 14 family lines that gave themselves over to gods of this world. These 14 families are called the purebloods. They are the ones that sold themselves and the souls of all their ancestors into the service of Satan. They have dissociated their children through trauma, sexual abuse/incest and the worship of various gods of this world, all in order to continue the family line. They are the progenitors of the Nephilim.

A clan is generally composed of those who are pureblood; these are classified as being alpha carriers. They have a blood line that dates back to one of the original families at the tower of Babel. They come from every corner of the world since each and every language on the earth will have someone from the tower of Babel as their founder. The alpha is a term that means the original carrier of the curse or disease of that particular familiar entity and that one that has the potential to pass it onto another person. They are born with the entity, attached at the genetic level.

A beta is someone that has received the curse or familiar entity but that does not have the potential to pass it onto another person. They receive the entity after birth. The beta can be incorporated into the family line through marriage to a pureblood. The idea of clan continuance and domination happens through the marriage between families and the inclusion of non-purebloods from each family. In every family there will be those who are rulers and those that are slaves. The slave will usually be given to marry a non-pureblood in order to bring them into the family line. The non-pureblood is called a blue blood because they have willingly made an agreement to give themselves and their children over to the god of this world. By making this agreement they are brought under the wings of Lucifer and their children are guaranteed a place in the kingdom of darkness. The spouse will be able to have a dominating throne placed in them but they will not have a Nephilim. The children of the pureblood and blueblood will have Nephilim. This is a generational lineage curse of transcendence originating from an ancestor that was either, somehow cursed or themselves made a pact with an entity which would affect them and all of their descendants with the curse of the animal spirit or other type of spirit.

Another example of these are those who willingly take the mark of the beast and then have it transmitted unto their children giving them the internal dwelling of the spirit of the beast which will have the ability to take over their mind at times causing them to fugue while the spirit of the beast possesses their mind and body. All purebloods do this to their children. Fugue is a mental episode where time stops for the individuals conscious and while they are absent from the conscious mind another personality or entity controls their mind and body. Man is made in the image of God so the greatest act of defiance and rebellion is to give oneself over to the complete control of the beast. The parents willingly have the mark of the beast and so before the child is ever conceived they have given it over to Satan and have asked it to be birthed with his mark upon it.

When the beast takes over the person they will be in a state of fugue allowing the entity to do whatever they desire with the person's body. When a holy prostitutes body is being used for bestiality they are often in a state of fugue while the beast is using their body to perform coitus with the animal. Just like Nebuchadnezzar was completely given over to being an ox, the person that the beast rises up in will become in mind, body and soul an animal. It will then perform he acts of sexual debauchery. When they have the mind of the beast they will lose all aspects of humanity becoming an animal. The mind of the beast falls into two categories: those who can control the spirit and those who lose all control to it. The spirit can manifest in these two ways:

> ➤ **Lunacy-** The person with the curse of lunacy loses all aspects of humanity and completely takes on the form and actions of an animal. It is called lunacy because it was believed that the goddess of the moon had possessed the mind of the individual transforming their mind into that of an animal. This type of possession only affects their mind. Their body does not change but they will act and do

everything just like an animal. They will have sexual acts with other animals and will act just like the animal they have become. I have personally seen this while working in the prison system. There was a man that would believe he was a wolf every time the moon came out. In order to protect him the guards would place him in a padded room before any full moon. This was to keep him from hurting himself. I remember the first time I saw this man. As I watched him I said to myself that he was completely out of his mind. He was sitting on his hunches and howling at the moon through the little window at the top of the wall. He would go about on all fours like a dog, growling and scratching at imaginary fleas. The next day the man awoke with no remembrance of the night before not even remembering that he had been locked up for attacking a person while in the mind of the animal. When possessed, he would be incredibly ferocious and vicious. His strength would increase beyond a human's natural abilities. The psychiatrist equated it to the amount of adrenaline in his system.

> ***The furrier-*** The furrier takes on some aspects of an animal like increased hair and nail growth with muscle and stature adaptation. The furrier will have increased physical abilities such as agility, strength, constitution, hearing, and vision. They may also experience changes in their dietary preferences such as craving meat, blood or even grass depending upon the creature they become. The Bible tells of Nebuchadnezzar being changed into an ox and living for seven years in the form of an ox.[167] While in the form of an ox he lived entirely on grass and plants that he grazed on. He was a furrier.

Whether the spirit manifests in lunacy or the furrier the Clan is a community that is not common. Clans will usually dwell in locations that are reclusive or in areas that are remote and not easily accessible to the general populace. When they are a clan that worships a goddess such as

---

[167] Daniel 4:30-ff. King James Version of the Holy Bible

Diana or Isis they will lead normal lives as active parts of society but they will lead a double life. They will practice all forms of incest, bestiality, and witchcraft. One this all clans have in common is that tThey will usually have incestuous relationships that may include the practice of bestiality. Because of the immense amount of energy that a shape shifter gets from the entity dwelling in them, they will have a retarded aging process. This is due to their inherent ability to regenerate new tissues after each transformation. Furrier may transform in mind only to an animal for the purpose of bestiality. The parts of the body that are damaged from the sexual acts will be   regenerated quickly so there is little or no evidence of what has taken place. Realize that the furrier, the one possessed by the mind of the animal for the purpose of bestiality, will not know what they were involved in nor will they have any memory of the events that have transpired. Each day will begin anew day for them.

The changeling that is a beta is a morph that has become infected by an alpha through sexual interaction or by being joined through an unholy union of some sort. This is called an unholy tie. A beta can also be the result of a curse. There are rare cases when a person gets cursed from an item. Unlike furriers a beta body does not have a slowed aging effect nor does their body have the ability to regenerate complete tissue replacements. Conversely their bodies will age and degenerate at an increased rate which worsens with each metamorphic transformation. The life of a beta is often filled with fear and a sense of helplessness and hopelessness. They will have an inner fear that they are cursed. Even though they may not understand curses, a beta knows deep inside something is not right and for this cause will often seek counseling or help.

A person can be set free from everything listed in this book. It does not matter what you or your family have been involved in the true God has made a way for you to be saved and set free from the curse of sin. All angels bow to the authority of the true God. No angel can own you; if you believe this than you have been lied to. Jesus Christ paid for you when he shed his blood. He not only created every person but he also came to earth and paid the price for their sins.[168] He shed his blood in order to cleanse you from all sin. He can heal your broken heart and can integrate your mind making you whole. Will you please call upon him today? I am available for consultation and can be contacted through my website via email or you can call my phone.

---

[168] Colossians 1:16; Galatians 3:3; 1 Peter :8; 1 John 2:2; John 3:16-23; Romans 10:9-13

The number is on the website. I pray the Lord richly bless and keep you in His will as you endeavor to serve Him.

In Christ's love: Dr. Tom Knotts, Jr.

www.SRA-DIDFreedomInChrist.com

www.ingramcontent.com/pod-product-compliance
Lightning Source LLC
Chambersburg PA
CBHW071357310526
45789CB00020B/456